Go West or Die

1907 - 1988
Lazarus Kundozeroff

Go West or Die

A biography of Lauri Kuntijärvi
- an edited version of his original text

Kaarina and David Worsley

Published in Great Britain 2021
by K&D

© Kaarina and David Worsley
Translated by Kaarina Worsley
Published by K & D Worsley
Cover design by authors

Printed and bound by CPI Group (UK) Ltd,
Croydon, CR0 4YY

ISBN 978-1-9996779-2-3

CONTENTS

CONTENTS	v
INTRODUCTION	vi
LAURI'S LIFE - IN HIS OWN WORDS	8
GOING TO SCHOOL	29
FUTURE - WRITING OR JOURNALISM?	41
THE WINTER WAR - 1939	55
RAGNAR NORDSTRÖM	75
HOW TO ARRANGE CIVILIAN LIFE	83
WRITING IS BETTER THAN FARMING	105
A NEW BEGINNING	117
A NEW PATH	125
NOW I LIVE ALONE	135
WE START OUR RESEARCH	140

INTRODUCTION

I had flown back to Helsinki in a hurry, but the plane was late. My father passed away as the wheels touched down. My two brothers and I thought that he was an ordinary dad. We could not have been more wrong!

When we return from the funeral, a man asked for permission to speak at the wake. Said 'yes', but wondered who he was? He was the baby who escaped with his mother and Lauri.

What? Escaped? from where? from whom? A new story for me and for many who were present.

Later at the flat, I open a large cardboard box, which is full of papers. A letter catches my eye. It starts "Uncle Kuntijärvi" - dated 10/3/1945 Loviisa. She is asking Uncle to help her with a job application. Who is this young girl?

The letter is from a boarding school called Sampola in Loviisa. It is not a boarding school as you know it in England. She is one of the children whose parents have escaped from Karelia and now live and study here, or the family has no money, or they are orphans. Helped by wealthy Karelians or state funding.

I am mystified - my mind is spinning/excited. I must look into this sometime.
Kaarina.

THE Back story

Soukelo (66N/33E), where Lauri was born, is just south of the Arctic. Temperatures vary from +25 to -25, sometimes colder. (During the Winter War, the temperature fell to -43 degrees). Daylight is enough to read by for approx 2 to 23 hours per day depending on cloud cover.

March 8th, 1917: The Bolshevik Revolution started. The communist Lenin took power.

December 6th, 1917: Finland declared independence from Russia. The border 1340 km long was closed by the Russians causing the Finns to commandeer homes on or close to the border to accommodate border guards until Border Posts were built.

At Soukelo, some inhabitants saw smoke from a fire. They were curious. Who could it be, friend or foe? They cautiously approached and waved a white flag. It turned out that they were Finnish soldiers. Friends! The soldiers asked if there were red soldiers in the village. As the answer was 'no' the Finns were invited back to rest and eat. Jenni went to the neighbouring village of Ruva 8km away to find out the situation. As a suitable excuse, Jenni took the pattern of a coat to a cousin who was a tailor.

Yes, the cousin was found but the piece of cloth Jenni had "forgotten at home". However, it was soon clear that there were no Reds in the village, and Jenni took this information back to the Finnish soldiers. After eating and resting they left on their skis.

The Berlin Wall fell in 1988 - less than twelve months after his death.

LAURI'S LIFE - IN HIS OWN WORDS

> *"Karelians are like fine plants, the weaker ones will need planting in good soil. This is because, they are rare, and only a few exist now"*

My father caused a problem when he returned from service in the Tsar's navy. In the rural villages, there were no social positions. The inhabitants' welfare was based on their diligence in collecting the yield of nature. In some patriarchal families, if there was a dispute leading to a central family quarrel, the solution was either: they eventually agreed; or one of the brothers (and his wife) left his former childhood home. In this way a new house was created in the village.

My father, Mehvo, a robust man who had an extraordinarily fine character had fallen into the employ of the Tsar of Russia where he served as a sailor for seven years. When he returned home to Kuntijärvi, his older brother argued about the division of the land and houses. Mehvo had not worked in the fields nor at the maintenance of their house for seven years. His brother demanded that this should be a consideration. Father said "If the Tsar could hear you, you would serve the rest of your life in

Modern day examples of the household items made from birch bark by the villagers

prison. Good bye". He left everything and went to another village - Soukelo - a village with fourteen houses.

There, he was married and given some land as a dowry and houses. I believe he also built houses. I remember two in different places around the lake. This is where my father lived with my small mother. He was quiet, but in the navy he had learned different things, some languages, Russian of course, Scandinavian and some English - a sailor learns necessary words only, so it was probably very little. There wasn't much company for a world traveller. The village only had the good book, and only the Kirjanainen - ´the book woman' had other languages. It follows that he found companionship from his life-companion at home. He could read, so this remote village perhaps did not offer much company or excitement to him. They shared the life as it was, and had five children.[1]

During the years of the peace the life went fairly comfortably. The bread of half a year was obtained from the fields, the second half was brought from the shore of the White Sea in the winter with a sleigh and a boat in the summer. There were the fish and game enough. But it was different during the bad times.

I remember that my mother fell into the ice covered lake, but was rescued. It was very cold and Jevdokia was taken very ill and became blind. She said to Mehvo, her husband, that he should take another woman. "I am not able to look after the house and children". Blind and perhaps also paralysed. I do not remember this exactly.

So Mehvo took another woman to the house and had two more children with her. The children were called Stepanie, Leontie,

---

1 It is likely that he shared stories of his time in the navy and the different ports that he had visited with his children.

Lauri's home is "Leontie Kuntijärven talo"

Uljana, Lauri (born 20/3/1906), Okahvie and Hekla and Vaseli. The last two were step siblings of Lauri.

My home village had neither a school nor other culture buildings. There was a tsasouna[1] so our souls were taken care of. Verses from the good book were read sometimes in the cottage, or sometimes in the tsasouna. Particularly the tsasouna was used in the summer.

The people's poetry also lived. "Tarpoi nuotan tappuraksi" was a known song in the village and it was sung particularly when setting nets on fishing trips. I also knew all of these verses.

In the living room of the farmhouses games were played but I didn't know them nor was I accepted as a partner, but I was there as part of the group. The life of my village included fishing and the hunting of game, and making household objects out of the bark of the birch. Out of doors we played games, such as Kyykkä[2].

As far as education is concerned, there was no school in the village. Later, a school was started in the another village. Teaching was in Russian but Paavo Ahava and other friends brought to the Karelian villages a small book "Pieni Alkuopas" from which we learned some Finnish.

Soukelo in 1918 the village led the primitive life of a forest village. Every house in the village had their own small plot in which barley, potato, turnips, onions et cetera were cultivated. The rye was sown only by the house of Tiittala. When the serial harvest was insufficient for the whole year, flour had to be brought. In the summer this was by the boat along the lakes and rivers waterways. Where the water ways did not connect, then they used portage.

---

1 *Eastern Orthodox village chapel*

2 *Finnish skittles*

In 1918 the village was stressed by a severe flour shortage. The bread made from bark or straw were quite generally eaten. There were 1-5 cows per house. In the summer the cattle got its food from the natural pastures and the winter food was harvested from meadows. The meadows were around the shorelines of both villages and there were grasslands to the west of the village that were cleared by the villagers. A few houses had reindeer. The biggest herd comprised 500 heads. The reindeer were grazed to the west of the village in some wooded hills. The cattle were grazed on the shores of lakes. White fish (laverets) were farmed in the waters of the lake.

One can hardly talk of the culture of the village without referring to the Kalevala. Kullervo's youth was sung about on the fishing trips. The shanty "Tarpoi" was used to give rhythm to the fishing. Where a school was missing, the illiteracy was general, but we did have a "The book woman" in the village. She read the slavonic Bible on the religious occasions arranged on holy days.

FINLAND'S CIVIL WAR SPREADS

In 1918 times became restless. Finnish red[1] guardsmen appeared in the village, one of whom was nick-named "Sinipuksu[2]." He functioned as some kind of agitator. In the Spring, there were armed men about whose actions the villagers had no clear picture. As time past, however, it became clearer. The Whites made two attacks from Finland to the village. After the second attack the Reds of the village fled but the attackers also withdrew. During the first attack the old man of the house of Seredin was hit in his chest by a bullet while hiding in the cellar. The Reds said

---

1 *Reds were communist followers, Whites socialists*
2 *'Blue trousers'*

that the old man had been siding with the whites. They shot their own man.

After these raids the Reds left the village but they often made patrol trips searching for food. In turn the villagers hid during the nights in the forests which were to the west, such as the forest cabins. The village also took its food provisions into the forests. This spring and summer the village was empty for long periods. During the day they went to the village to work, and returned into the forests at night.

It became obvious that the trend of the inhabitants of the village was to the west, except that in addition there were hiding places in the forests of the west side of the village. It is to be noted that during wartime year of 1922 a great number of the inhabitants of the village emigrated to Finland.

MY WAR

My war was short. But there were stages in it. There was shortage of bread in this village in the spring of 1921 and probably in other North Karelian villages. My father managed the matters of the family and in connection with these arrangements he made a short trip to Finland's Paanajärvi in Kuusamo. He took me with him to Paanajärvi and left me in a big house where I worked for my food. In this way I was separated from my father, but in the autumn, he for some reason, moved me to the other end of the lake into a smaller house. Before Christmas I left for Karelia with a voluntary group who were a white liberation army which had come from Sohjana. In Oulanka I became the battle messenger for the chief of the unit. Then warlike work began. In Oulanka we did field exercises for some time, I ran and skied carrying the chief's orders in different directions to the chiefs of battle units.

The war was comfortal
One day hostilities k
brought a message that
Our patrol opened fire a
sleigh had ambled back
come.

The Ruva civilians ga
from there towards Mu
memories of that time a
we proceeded from Oula
we progressed we took o

My chief asked - or ra'
ordered to go out to
not occur to any
back village
I repo
drink
se

including Soukelo, my home village. I was allowed to leave a small amount of meat and flour at my home. I have no memory of what kind of "war hero" I was considered at home and how I behaved. As far as I can recall, the relationships in the family had been always good, but now the joy of a meeting and reunion was at its height.

Only father had a knowledge of the state of the war at large. The following morning he came with us as we started off to Ruva. We arrived at the village just after midnight, and took lodgings in the village left by the enemy in the belief that during the following day we would continue the enemy's chase, but it turned out otherwise.

The enemy had met a Finnish skiing group, who had come from Murmansk, in the village of Kananainen. There, the chief of the Murmansk group shot the chief of the enemy and the enemy retreated to the village of Ruva - the village from which it had just left, to which we had come in the small hours.

The encounter began. We were having a morning tea when someone came in and announced "There's shooting outside".

er ordered - "The battle messenger is
ok for who is shooting and at what". It did
e of us that an enemy would have come to the
m which it had retreated only couple of days ago.
d that the fighting was going on and we left without
g tea. Once outside, the chief and battle messenger were
parated from each other. He was able to flee in the groups which
will withdraw at some stage. I was taken a prisoner, and my father
fell.

A BEREAVED PRISONER

My war at this stage ended here. I found myself as a prisoner
in the hands of the chief of the Reds - driving his sledge. The
chief told me that he had encountered my father during the attack
in open battle and he (the chief) had fired first. "It could have
ended differently" the Red guard said.

We travelled. Winter days passed. There was bright snow and
the conifers green but in my mood there was neither light nor
hope. It was January and dark.

Then my fate was changed onto a strange route. The further
away from the fighting we travelled the more relaxed they became,
and the more I was ignored. As we approached the Murmansk
rail track I fell from their attention until we arrived at the rail
track. There, I was transferred to the men delivering logs. This
work force were Karelians, men and horses delivering logs. To my
astonishment I found my brother and our horse were working
there. The Reds had commandeered the horses to take a Russian
detachment to the front and I was put as driver of my own horse.
The enemy had placed me in charge of my own horse! We went
back to the front, to those same villages from which I had just

It was in Ruva that Mehvo was shot, and Lauri taken prisoner 10th January, 1922.

*The dotted line is the retreat of the bolsheviks with Lauri
Source: Map is ASK 1934. KSS archives.*

come. After a while by a field my horse became tired. It was driven to one side, the load redistributed to the other loads, and so I was left with my tired, exhausted horse on the spring ice.

I allowed my horse to stand still for hours. I found a little hay in the sleigh, fed it, then when the enemy had vanished from view, I began to lead my horse with a handful of hay. The trip progressed slowly but the destination was the village of Soukelo and home. To my surprise the horse survived on the pastures during a lean spring and gained weight in my brothers' good hands.

When I arrived back home after my war experiences I learned that the men of our village had all fallen - according to the red Finns. They told each woman how her husband had been killed so that the "better" stories would be believed.

I made a sortie to Finland along the backwoods and brought back the welcome news that all were well and I had talked to some of them. I had met them in the attic of the granary of a house where I was staying. This attic was my consulting room in which I met the men and received messages to be taken to the women of the home village.

One of them, Jenni the wife of Haukilahti, made me promise that when I leave for Finland permanently then I must take her as well. I promised.

One day a man called Musta-Olli, a family relative, arrived from Kostovaara and said that a group from Oulanka was coming to arrest me, Jussi and others. In addition to my other bad deeds, the communists of Paanajärvi had reported my last couple of visits to Oulanka in Finland and my actions there, and it had been decided to imprison me. It was not possible to justify these acts with the fact that I was young. This excuse was okay during the war because of the circumstances but now the trips to Finland could not be justified.

Flight was unavoidably in front of me, and it had to be made that very night because according to the narrator the captors would arrive tomorrow.

I talked with Jussi and we agreed the matter. The third man, Mikitä, who also had to leave was at that moment too sleepy and we could not wake him. We left him at home to sleep. His family was fishing that night. Although he was a relative I do not know what happened to him.

The fishing people began to return to home shores in the the small hours. The women of Mikkilä (a house nearby) also returned and amongst them was mistress Haukilahti (Jenni). My moment had come. I went to Mikkilä by rowing over the home bay, and greeted Oksieni (Jenni's sister-in-law) on the shore. I explained that I was the searching for Jenni because a cow had sprained an ankle and it needed attention.

Jenni had already gone but Oksieni called her back. I had only to say to her that now it is time to leave. We will meet at the mouth of the river. I also, of course, talked about the sprained ankle of the cow. I rowed over the bay and I left my own boat by the shore of Mikkilä and then walked along the shore to my home. The home bay was very calm that night. Later, I saw Jenni rowing the boat towards our shore, with a small boy in the boat. She had taken her sleeping son this night time to "treat the cow". Oksieni must have guessed the purpose of the trip and perhaps they said their goodbyes at this significant hour of parting, I never asked. My own separation from my home took place quickly. I came back in the small hours, greeted the sleepy and said goodbye to my sisters. Somehow there was half a loaf in my hand for lunch on the trip and then I left. Only the hinge creaked when I shut the door the last time.

We four I, Jussi, Jenni and her small boy met each other in the mouth of Heinäjoki. With Jussi we went to Jenni's boat and rowed along Heinäjoki (a river) as far as we could. We drew the boat to the land and we left along the track towards Finland's border. We headed for Murtokumpu which I had visited before and onto Viinikumpu on the Finnish side. Our progress succeeded well. Sometimes the boy had to be carried but it did not hamper our trip.

We arrived at the border. Jussi and I hastened quickly over the no man's land, as the danger of the being noticed was greater than in the forest. And besides, the border guards probably patrolled near the border. Jenni did not think of this. She had other matters in her mind. In the middle of no man's land she turned towards Karelia and made the sign of the cross. Perhaps she did this three times, and then bowed towards Karelia with deep conviction. After this, she stepped onto foreign land holding the hand of her son. She was now a refugee of Karelia as were we all.

In the evening we arrived at a house on Finland's side at about 18 o'clock, which was about 2 km from the border at the bottom of lake Paanajärvi. A discussion was had about going to the house, we were all tired, but did not know who occupied it. When we entered we found out. The Finnish border guards were there! They received us kindly. They told that the foreign patrol had moved on the countrys' border just a moment ago along the route that the refugee group had only just walked. It was lucky for the group that it did not crash into the patrol. The saving factor was

Finnish / Russian Border

Russian officials reportedly stopped more than 1,000 people from illegally crossing the border into Finland in 1918, according to the Lännen Media news consortium.

that a member of the group had needed to have a small rest, which they had taken away from the road.

The Finnish guards telephoned their office in Kuusamo and reported that four border defectors had come to them. They were told that the defectors must be returned back behind the border immediately. While hearing this, Jenni was looking west towards Paanajärvi and saw a boat was coming towards them. Jenni suggested that they await the arrival of the boat which will be soon. The boat arrived and in it there were two Finnish soldiers one of whom was a captain. The guards reported to the captain that here are 4 refugees who were ordered to return across border. The captain was unaware of them. He telephoned Kuusamo. He said that these refugees must be first interrogated. They should be taken to Kuusamo for this interrogation. It was decided that they have to walk. Jenni as the oldest of the group agreed. She added that neither the lunches nor their money was weighing them down.

We had three guards. Our journey continued by rowing along Paanajärvi. This was about 20 km. We were happy to row during that evening and arrived at the western head of the lake at about 21 o'clock. From there, the captain phoned the rural police chief at Kuusamo and said that the refugees are arriving by foot. Jenni estimated that it was about 80km.

The following day after walking for more than 5 hours, we came to an unknown house. Jenni suggested to the guards that perhaps we could rest in this house. Going into the house they were greeted "Oh my goodness, the little woman" - (the height of Jenni was 147cm).

He asked the guards if he could talk to the refugees. He spoke for a while on the phone to the rural police chief of Kuusamo, asking that he should look after these runaways with food and

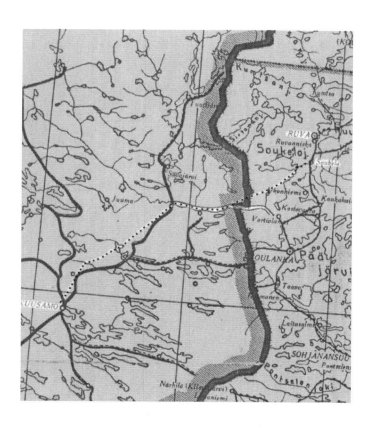

The dotted line shows the escape route from Soukelo: through the forest to the border; west along Paanajärvi lake; south west from there to Kuusamo

water, and that he would come the next morning. He was adamant that under no circumstances should we be sent back. When he got off the phone, he confirmed the arrangements he had made with the guards and group. He repeated that these refugees must not be sent back under any circumstances. The runaways did not look very dangerous anymore because the number of the guards was reduced to one.

The walk lasted all day long and ended in the jail at Kuusamo. We were given bread, fish and water. We did not meet the local chief again. The original guard was replaced with a new one who was very talkative. During the following day he invited us to the barracks to look at the people coming to a dance - did we recognise anyone? We did not, so the guard showed us a big bunch of photographs. Jenni found two familiar Viena Karelian women.

During the morning the rural police chief and the police came to interrogate us. They interrogated only for a little while. Then the guard said that now we leave for the house of Risti-Jussi to meet the women that they had recognised in the photos. We were given food and drink. The women were there. Together, the entire group including the guard, went to the famous Karelian shopkeeper, Paavo Ahava who was originally from Uhtua. He knew Jenni, and he offered Jenni a loan of FIM 500 for a car journey to Oulu. Jenni thanked for the offer but refused. She knew that the trip can be made in another way.

Jenni knew about her husband that he was logging somewhere at Ii river. The group continued towards the west, to Taivalkoski. There they went into the house of the Karelian shopkeeper Jakoleff. To her joy, Jenni found her husband waiting for her and after their tearful reunion the family went on their new path.

The journey from Kuusamo was to be continued by bus as far as Taivalkoski and then to Oulu. But I had never heard of nor seen a bus. Waiting for it were the men that I had met in the granary attic at Paanajärvi. They explained to me that the bus is like a house, or room. I waited excitedly for the Karelian cottage to come round the corner!

When it arrived it was neither a Karelian nor Finnish cottage but a bus - one that we all now know.

Jussi and I continued our trip to Oulu on the bus, and began dreaming of our own separate futures. I had neither seen nor imagined a place with so many houses and people. My journey continues to a place where I will learn many things. I had never been to a school before. So a new period in my life is about to start.

We lived in a two story log house with men from different villages in Karelia, men who were working in logging camps. There were only men, who cooked, ate bread and American lard or bacon. Evening would be playing cards, perhaps drinking, somebody tried to arrange their herbarium ready for autumn term. These were men who had lived in their own houses, owners of land in Viena (county in Karelia), but now because change in circumstances worked in a logging camp - where the village was hostile towards them.

One evening we had a Karelian themed event which was arranged as a play[1]. This was perhaps an early club event by Karelians themselves. I could not read at this time, but attended anyway. One evening a very important man was speaking to us. His speech was serious. "They (bolsheviks) are trying to lure you back - with a promise of amnesty. You must not believe it, you will

_____

1 *A Karelian wedding as a play.*

"Neither a Karelian nor Finnish cottage - but a bus"
Notice the horse and sleigh in the background

end up in jail". I had escaped a jail threat already once, so I would not even think about it.

During this evening I met a boy from my village. He had applied to a new refugee school, which was starting this autumn. He had a place. After a long talk we decided that I should also apply, all good because I was also accepted. So in the autumn we two boys from Soukelo started our learning, sixteen years old and starting from the beginning.

GOING TO SCHOOL

MY FIRST SCHOOL - AT MAIKKULA

School started first in a farmhouse, but later moved to prison buildings. So I am in a prison but not as a prisoner. The old cells were our dormitories, there was also a dining area, all this had a barbed fire fencing around it - perhaps from the jail time, we were not planning to escape. Outside the fencing was a building were the headmaster and teachers lived. Their building was in a nice park. The middle room was for assembly and detention for pupils.

I was once in detention. Maybe justified, but I did not think so. Some boys had bought copper pipe to make a rifle. It was used to shoot into the outside loo for target practice, and if anybody was inside at the time it would have been dangerous. So maybe the punishment was justified. Others had apologised, but I could not do so, because this time I had not been there. I had been on the trip to buy the copper tube earlier. It was getting late, the young teacher tearfully suggested that maybe I could apologise for some other event and this could wipe out both things. I realised that we

Lauri is seated on the right

were both correct. This was not crime and punishment, but two different personalities, both right in their own way. It was her job as a teacher to keep discipline and for me a young man who already had a lot of experience, to accept our roles. We parted company finally.

At school many children were younger than us. We had to master the ABC and to read etc. Spelling was hard, but when you get it, everything became easier. I progressed with my studies - not the most talented, at least three were better than me in maths, I knew more history than other boys. Maybe my talent was in performing arts. The school started a Karelian Club, I became the chairman, why I have now idea. I spoke, a person recited a poem or a story was read and so on.

Life was not all sunshine for me, dark clouds were gathering. One day headmaster called me in told me I had to leave the school, to take all my belongings and report to the head office at Oulu. I had said something against him. Whilst waiting for food we had spoken loudly and said they should not call us Russians. That was all, but it was no good. I gathered my meagre belongings and started walking, Oulu was about 8 kilometres distance. The headmaster had been used to prison discipline and carrying his bunch of prison keys, so he was a very firm man in his opinions, the pleading of the staff and pupils was no use. When I arrived at Head Office they were ready to send me back to Kuusamo to my parents. I explained that my mother had died a long time ago, my father was shot at Ruva campaign where I was taken a prisoner. I had nothing to do with Kuusamo, I worked at the logging camp at Ii during the summer.

A phone call to the school was a success, but with the advice "to be obedient to the headmaster, we believe that your teachers

My end-of-year speech at Lahti - 1926-27

We have been wandering under a heavy burden, Karelian youth, from place to place. Tired from it all, we have been able to stop here to gain new strength for the next part of our journey. Now we must part and leave our beloved "home". We are going our separate ways, inside you may feel sad and glad. Sad, because you are leaving friends and this place you regarded as your home. But glad as you return to hearth and home, where your earliest childhood memories are. Most of you have your parent's love waiting for you. You can tell them all, joys and worries - what has happened during this season. Parents love and home is best, if only we could fully understand it.

However, not everybody has been able to spend their childhood at home. We refugees, have to accept our orphan state. All the things that a home, the nature around there, once offered us, are only memories in our mind.

At a place of learning, here in Lahti, at this college, we have been prepared for life. To get here, we faced many difficulties. Here the feeling of our nation, the Karelian tribe, lives very strongly, maybe stronger than anywhere else.

We, who have lived here a year, understand that work, which is based on love and understanding, will do. Elsewhere, where demonstrations against us have happened, make us realise the importance of your work. We have been allowed to bring forth our talents, and even the tribal question was allowed - celebrating a festival. It shows that, we have not been treated as strangers or enemies.

There have been nineteen Karelians here, but even this large number has not stopped you helping and understanding us, both in spiritual and material ways.   Lauri Kuntijärvi like you". The return was a happy one. The teachers started special plans for us older boys, and as a result we became so clever that 3 terms were passed in one semester. In the spring we could leave the school with a certificate. We had passed 6 years of the primary school in a record time. I was given a small Greek statue as present from staff as the chairman of the club.

FURTHER EDUCATION

My friend went to agricultural college, so why I came to this school in Lahti I have no recollection. It was like a high school. We had lessons, plenty of studying on your own, problem solving and discussions within a group. In front of your peers you had to present and talk about a subject. I passed some subjects to high school level and history was a particularly good for me. I noticed that my memory was not so good but logic was, and when given various details, it was easy for me to arrange them into a logical pattern. I could also speak easily and had a voice, so the fiery speaker was born. I was asked to speak, and later to write about the event.

I was in Lahti for two years, but what now. This was not a school where you learned a profession. It was for students, who needed to broaden their general education. I sent my application with the headmaster´s recommendation to Sortavala, a teaching seminary.

Once school ended and while waiting for the new school, I needed to earn money. The man from Soukelo at the logging camp helped me, sent the money for the journey. I could live with them and work. However now that I had started 'book' learning covering many subjects, and I really enjoyed it all. I had to have more and more of it.

The first school that I applied to did not offer a place, what to do next? Karelian students at Lahti suggested that I should apply to this new school in Helsinki - a university college which later became Tampere University. But there was a problem. Money to pay for my fees and living costs for the whole term?

On a sunny day in August at the logging camp, two events happened that had a significant impact on my life. Some letters, and the boss Pekkala. I received a letter signed by Yrjö Ruutu, who was head of the college. I was accepted.

At lunch time, I talked with others from Karelia. The ability to read was important to me, but they did not understand, it was a skill that they did not have.

At the end of the lunch, the boss approached me, read the letter and spoke very firmly. "Of course you must go, the world is full of money", and in that moment it was decided. I would go, no ifs or buts, just go.

Next day the local tailor made me a new suit. My savings from previous years mounted to 6000 marks (in 1926 and it is about 1630 Euros in 2006). Previously, I had food and bed in both schools, and a stipend in Lahti , so I must believe his words - the world is full of money. This is an important moment in my life, I am moving to Helsinki, which is a very large city. I had no knowledge of the place and I shall be on my own.

I MOVE TO HELSINKI

The school was demanding, and I was regarded as a clever student, but I knew from before that memory related matter was hard. Learning a foreign language with it's vocabulary, was not for me. Why? When young, learning songs whilst fishing had been easy. Hear it once and I could remember it. But however hard I tried, language learning was a failure. Yet politics, economics, history of literature and writing were no problem. I gained the highest marks possible (straight A's). I wrote informal articles, which I could send to and be paid by the Helsingin Sanomat[1].

However, money became a problem. To my great sadness, the East-Karelian committee, which received money from the Government Refugee Fund, did not accept me on the list. So no money from them. Their reasoning was that money was only given for early learning not for my level of studies. If no help was forthcoming, I had to find it on my own.

Worries, yes I had them during school time. I remembered the words of the communist at the logging camp, "The world is full of money", but uncertainty was often in my mind.

The Karelian club continued weekly meetings. Membership was a mix of society from domestics, small shop keepers, students and so on. These were people who could improvise poetry, for instance if they forgot lines, they made up their own. But this was a group who were not yet able to create a nation or a state. They had moved from southern parts of Karelia singing their songs until they met an insurmountable border, the Arctic Ocean. Well, Viena was a nice enough place to live in until it was denied to us and we had to move again to Finland.

Our common heritage was obvious, and clearly different from the new country, where everybody was from our own country was a relative and a friend. After an evening of a party, sewing circle, or choir it could continue further. A walk home, maybe even an invitation for a coffee in the flat. Our tribal customs were fairly strict on this so if you waited too long perhaps you ended up a

---

1 *A daily newspaper like Times or Telegraph in the UK*

spinster - on the shelf. I met Anni, who became my wife later - perhaps in the choir.

Actual organisation of the clubs happened eventually. They were really youth clubs with educational ideas. These were all over Finland, wherever enough Karelians lived a club was founded. Eventually a central body was arranged. Many smaller ones did not have to register as long as the central body knew about them.

A PLACE TO LIVE

The school address was very close to the main station and theatre in Helsinki and I found a place to live close by. So all is well.

My subjects and teachers were: journalism by Yrjö Soini; political science Yrjö Ruutu; economics Dr Harmaja; law by Puhakka; and also literature. Languages included Finnish, Estonian and English. I made a mistake with a German and Russian names because of the alphabets[1] when I wrote about Karl Marx. This was however passed because I mastered it despite the little confusion of names.

I made some connections, Professor Lauri Kettunen[2] became a friend, we were both from the same area. Also, the head of the school was friendly towards me. His letter accepted me and I remember the signature, Yrjö Ruutu.

I had helped his new party in various ways, money was always needed. The author Juhani Konkka founded a new party. When he spoke about more bread for the workers, they shouted clearly, 'put the loaf on the table man'. However, it did not amount to much. I did some work on the paper and got some 'bread'.

---

1 *He started to learn to read at 16, and is now 21*

2 *Kettunen wrote a Finnish Grammar, published 1934*

The KSS[1] gave me a very small stipend. The secretary and an author Iivo Härkönen brought the money. He found me sitting on the bed and singing. I got the money and he got my signature and left. We met later many a time and became friends.

I almost managed. Money was now gone and Christmas was approaching. People would lend me money, I know, but my pride would not allow it. I had asked for a loan from the friend at the logging camp. He was in position to do so, but it had not arrived yet.

On Christmas Eve, I could see into the Orthodox church, and into people's flats. They were getting the festive table ready before going to church, and to feast after the service. I had only one mark 45 pennies for my feast. I might buy 3 buns (korvapuusti = box on the ear), but could not because I was 5 pennies short. The buns cost 50 pennies each.

I would not give up yet, and looked in pockets for those 5 pennies. The trouser pockets, waistcoat, jacket but no luck. Shops would close soon. In desperation I searched deeper. I found a hole and luck was with me. Here was something, looking for 5 pennies, I found a note instead. So I now had 50 marks! Christmas is saved. I rushed out to buy something or somewhere perhaps to eat. But by now everything was closed, and the evening and Christmas day was spent 'happily' drinking water. Happy because I felt safe - 50 marks in my pocket and the money coming from the friend. On Boxing Day I treated my self in a restaurant to a slap up dinner.

The spring term was okay, I managed my money better, and lessons were reasonable. With spring coming, it was now lighter, sunshine made it warmer, so I had new hope for the future. Earlier

---

1 *Karjalan Sivistysseura*

after school, work had been very varied, not academic at all. This time literary work was on the horizon.

Korvapuusti or Cinnamon Bun

Ingredients

5 dl milk

50 gr yeast, fresh or dry

1 egg

1 dl sugar

1 tbl cardamom

1 1/2 teaspoon salt

approx 900 gr (14 dl) of flour

150 gr butter

Filling

100 gr butter

1 dl sugar

2 tbl cinnamon

Mix the yeast in warm milk, add egg, sugar, cardamom and salt. Add flour gradually and almost last add soft butter. Dough can be soft, knead it until it no longer sticks in your hands. Let it prove for 20 minutes.

Knead the dough and divided into 2 pieces, roll each piece into 30 x60 pieces. Spread half of the soft butter on and sprinkle sugar and cinnamon (half). Next roll it and leave the seam side down. Cut at an angle into 16 pieces. Lift them up with smaller side on top. Next press the top down. Do the second piece the same way.

Brush with egg and cook 225C for 8 - 10 minutes.

*Korvapuusti or Cinnamon Buns.
The crystals in the bowl are sugar*

*His faithful and treasured 'friend' which he used to
the end of his life*

FUTURE - WRITING OR JOURNALISM?

Lahti, my second school place, was in a county which had about eighty youth clubs. The central body wanted to mark the twenty five years of its existence by publishing its history as well as making improvements to the working of the clubs. The headmaster of the Lahti school suggested that I should apply to the central body of the local youth clubs for the secretary's position. As the chairman of this organisation, he had influence on the choice of the candidate. This was my first real job, secretary to the organisation, as a writer, and an organiser and was permanent for at least one year. I had great help and advice from my mentors, the headmaster and a teacher from the Lahti school.

The summer meant travelling from one club to another, where I rummaged through their minutes of the meetings and annual reports. The result was a two hundred and fifty page book which was published in Helsinki 1931. It was my first substantial publication.

During this time whilst collecting the information, their problems, I gave speeches which were followed by dances. This took three months and I was accommodated in farm houses where I slept in rarely heated guest rooms - and I couldn't possibly ask the girls to come and warm my bed. However, later I found a school teacher who was just as unhappy with her attic room. We teamed together for a moment and later parted as friends.

During this time I often had to visit the KKK[1] in Helsinki. The then Secretary, Takala, experienced the lack of funds and left to find a paying job. The next, Vallas Homanen, was a school friend of mine. The chairman leaves, another is elected, and now I was a member of the board and a deputy chairman. Like all societies, they were short of money and somehow we had to find more. To find enough money to pay for a secretary and postage etc.

All societies go through rough times, arguments, wrong people are chosen and so on. KKK was no different and times were hard, when you need people with a level head and clear ideas about finances. When the chairman dies, someone must replace him. I was familiar as a deputy, also very familiar with affairs of the clubs, because the time in Lahti had taught me a great deal. No advertising for a vacancy, anybody who can fill the post is accepted. I was that person, already in as the deputy.

I knew the financial situation well, so the first activity was - how to improve it. Earlier a communist had told me "the world is full of money" so long as you aim it for the right cause. We rented a small flat near centre of Helsinki by Stockman[2], the big department store. This was obviously an horrendous move, but more was to follow. We did not apply for money from organisations

---

1 *Karjalakerhojen Keskusliitto - central committee for the clubs*
2 *The Harrods of Finland*

Festival in Oulu 1935

which could tie us to them. Instead we started a paper and approached large commercial enterprises, state departments etc. who could place adverts. Lottery was also a good money earner. All this made our society very wealthy, and we could even donate money now.

An idea was developing in my mind about the government funding but the person and his friends who were making the decisions were from an other tribe, Inkeri. I decided to go to Viipuri (now part of Russia) and discuss the matter there. It was not the correct procedure. This was followed by a few long almost twenty four hour discussion with Reino Castren about the politics of the refugees. Luck was with me, we were able to arrange a meeting with Y. W. Puhakka (my former teacher here in Helsinki). He was now the Home Secretary in the government. His reply was not helpful - the civil servants know the matters and deal with them, I am only a temporary person there. After this somehow I was labelled a scoundrel or a villain, but we managed get a representative for the meetings. A secretary would have had more time, but my efforts had made me persona non grata.

Festivals were held in many locations, and eventually a program was developed and repeated all over Finland: a mixed choir made up of six choirs from the clubs amounting to almost one hundred singers, children dancing, sports events, and of course someone would speak.

We increased our activities by arranging courses where people could come and learn something new. When schools were on holiday and a place was empty for a week, it could be used by us or other people. I was able to arrange a second event at Maikkula which was my very first school. Arrangements done, others did the work and I just gave a speech at the end.

I had been elected as a member of the board of KSS in 1935, but this was nullified because I did not have Finnish nationality. This position was left vacant until the next annual meeting when Mikko Karvonen, a friend, was chosen.

Times were difficult, and our main object was to help members with advice and money. The families needed help in the new country and their children needed education.

One of several accounts of moneys received from Government Refugee funding committee and how and where spent	
Money received	17,500
Used Nurmijärvi grammar school	8,500
University and High school	3,000
Kemi High school	1,500
Kuopio vocational school	2,000
Ruukki Cookery school	500
Lapua Cookery school	2,000
Receipt for Lapua school to follow	_____
	17,500
Helsinki	May 5 1944
Secretary	Lauri Kuntijärvi
Editor	Lauri Kuntijärvi

VÄINÖLÄ - A NEW SCHOOL IDEA

The name was never really a problem, but finding a place was. My original idea was churning in my mind. It had to fulfil two criteria. In the summer it could be used as a summer place by prosperous Karelians, as well as their friends - fishing, a sauna and swimming, good Karelian food was also on my list of necessary things. It would be a holiday place and the money earned would be used in the winter for education.

This was really exciting, but I remembered my former teacher's advice. "Do not tell the world about a good idea it will be stolen. A fairly good one but not perfect will be laughed out of the room". I kept my mouth shut, and proceeded with my plans.

The location was important, if a school is already there it will help, a lake was needed for the summer in order to get people to come for a holiday and to pay for their stay. Kauniainen in Espoo was a Finnish speaking school which needed more pupils. A shallow lake was also on offer as well as being close to Helsinki, this was perhaps the best, but? The next area, Nurmijärvi, already had a Christian co-educational school and boarding school where the students lived, studied, ate, and slept. It was decided that we could gain experience here and then continue the idea for other schools elsewhere.

We started modestly in a rented house with a small number of pupils. Later, we received two houses from Sweden which were erected on six hectares of land that we bought from the parish church. We had a choice between two parcels of land, one of three hectares, the other six hectares. This choice caused heated discussions. On one side, the money was important, but the other side valued the opportunities that the larger offered. Of course, if you can have more and it is cheaper per hectare, some can only see the total price.

The meeting is worth mentioning. It was a nice sunny day, the board was present and discussing the purchase of the place. One man said, "if you buy this I will contribute 50, 000 marks". Everybody was eager to do the same, and offered various sums, but the

A work party preparing the ground for the arrival of the buildings from Sweden

first was the best. The meeting finished and no more was said of the donations, they disappeared into the blue sky.

Before the next meeting I had spoken with my friend and he was happy to place his donation on the table in cash at the meeting. Right in front of the chairman (Lauri Kettunen), Mikko said "We must keep our promises, so here is mine 10,000 marks". I noted it into the minutes of the meeting quickly. There were many surprised people round the table. I signed all the promises, one gave a cheque for 25,000 marks and the rest paid later as promised. One made his whole family a lifetime member and paid the sum, enquiring as he did so "do you think students will remember in years to come". I commented "No, perhaps not, but this way is good". Our project moved forward steadily.

We chose the larger plot, and the houses from Sweden were erected there. We were helped by university students to build the houses.

More for money, not always good. My idea was spoken also in a meeting in Viipuri. Privately it was noted an excellent idea, but if only it was somebody else. I knew I had an enemy in that camp, who later relented.

A friend who had helped me a number of times, needed some more students for a school he had started in Loviisa, his son wanted a Finnish education and none were available in the town. Only two more students were needed to qualify for a government grant - delivery time was two days. He got his students. Colonel Ragnar Nordström was a very special man, wealthy and a great Karelian friend, who had fought in early Karelian uprisings, I feel fortunate to have known him.

Our student numbers were increased to 25. To increase the number of university students was important. I believe that there

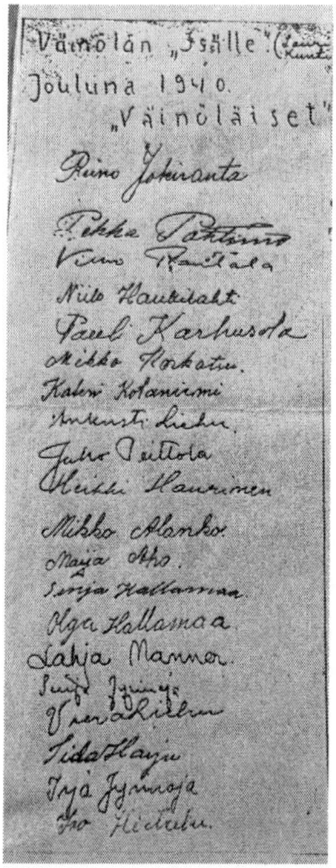

Väinölän „Isälle" (...
Jouluna 1940.
„Väinöläiset"

[handwritten list of signatures]

Greetings from the pupils to Lauri Kuntijärvi the "father" of Väinölä
Christmas 1940

> The letter requesting a place by Jenni's 'baby' who had escaped with Lauri.
>
> Karjalakerhojen Keskusliitto Helsinki
>
> I request permission to live in Koulukoti Väinölä (a place to live) which was founded for East Karelian refugees. I can pay my school fees, for food and lodging. I can pay 150 marks per month.
>
> Yli-Iissä 7/71941
>
> Respectfully Niilo Haukilahti

were only a couple of students who had received a higher degree. Ville Mattinen had started a foundation to help university students. Our aim was to get as many as possible to baccalaureate level[1], who could then apply for a grant. Nordström increased the size of accommodation for the students at Sampola, almost equalling the one in Väinölä. The same system was used here also. We arranged more students and at the beginning much of it was financed by Nordström. We founded also a vocational school where a variety of trades could be learned. Our biggest and most ambitious plan was a student house in Helsinki, where rents were huge and could put and end to their studies.

We tried to encourage families in various parts of Finland to send their children to school. It was a momentous event when a child from a humble background started school. The whole village would get encouragement and more children would apply for a place in Väinölä or Sampola, the two that we had founded.

Our Organisation had a remarkable success and received recognition for our work. The financial assistance which had been in

---

1 Higher than an A* or AS level

place in Viipuri was not functioning well anymore. My victory was that the hostile man was agreeable now to pass this task to our committee. Over a period of time we had become friends who understood each other. We achieved visibility, which was more important, higher education was now accepted. We knew that our people, the Karelian refugees, did not have an educated class, but one will develop from the children of the refugees if encouraged and given the opportunities.

The culture was beginning to show, writers, painters etc, but unfortunately war shattered it. Some had to escape to Sweden, here in Finland it stopped, even our school work ended.

The Association that I was working for was devoted to the refugees, and as such was forbidden under the Peace Treaty at the end of the war, and had to be abandoned. Some members of the committee understood this and worked speedily to prepare a replacement. This came in the form of a foundation which satisfied the long term needs.

The Association - its reputation and funds - was donated to a new body called Väinölä Foundation. The executive committee was chosen, without my knowledge, of people who were not of the right calibre. My people were still at the front fighting the war when the decision took place. I made it known that I could not agree. Jussi, whose dream was happening said "Could you not agree once with everybody? the country is in a state as well". I understood then, that our institutes would not work the same way after the war. Lauri Kettunen my former teacher and longstanding companion blamed me for not telling him about my stand on the matter. I was not aware of the arrangements which were made behind my back, that brought the foundation into being. I understood then it is better to leave.

The auction at the end of the Väinölä school

All was arranged by 23/2/1945. The Minister of Justice was Urho Kekkonen, who handled the matter in record time. Many associations were doomed in the Moscow Armistice 19/9/1944, which ended the Continuation War. So before the axe fell, the foundation was a reality, about four months before it was to be discontinued, like many a Karelian related matter.

I was starting a new project. Mrs Juurikainen, who had helped at Väinölä as matron and many other things was left high and dry. Her husband had died and she and a war orphan boy had nowhere to live. We raised money and, with a working group of volunteers, built a house. She raised her son to an academic level.

The land was eventually sold to Nurmijärvi council for 525,000 marks, and I am sad to say some of the money was used for statues. Not the original idea. The world has changed and will continue to do so.

A Finnish ski patrol in February 1940. SA-photo.

THE WINTER WAR - 1939

The Winter War began on the 30th November 1939, which was three months after WWII started. Russian forces were superior in strength but suffered heavy losses. Progress was slow. The Russian attack was regarded illegal by League of Nations and Soviet Union was expelled. The war lasted three months one week and six days. The Russian pre-war demands were huge because of the proximity of Leningrad, just twenty miles from the Finnish border. These demands were declined by the Finns, so USSR invaded. It is argued that their intention was to invade and take over Finland, but some sources deny it. The winter was severe with temperature was as low as -43 centigrade (-45.4F). Conditions were hard. The invaders changed their demands, which resulted in an expensive treaty for Finland; one percent of the territory was ceded. Finland kept her independence and increased her reputation round the world. The war was started without a declaration of war, which violated three non-aggression pacts. (Treaties of Tartu 1920, 1932, 1934). A hundred people killed and fifty buildings destroyed in Helsinki. Russian reply was, "We are not bombing, but giving humanitarian aid to the starving population".

An evacuation of 420,000 people is a massive problem for any country. The refugees left everything and now Finland had to find a way of supporting them. How to help them to merge into a Finnish society?

Our society still had hopes of returning to Karelia. The world events were not yet resolved, so maybe there was some hope. The everyday needs of our refugees of all ages was our main purpose now. Educating our countrymen was important, maybe if freedom became a reality, local people would be needed in the future. Our society was funding many students at both Väinölä and Sampola schools, where students lived and studied. In 1941-42 there were seventeen at Väinölä and twenty two at Loviisa. Other high schools had ten pupils assisted by us. Lower numbers than expected because the older students were in the armed forces and some did not return.

In the spring of 1942 a domestic economy course for twenty four girls took place at Väinölä for four months. The cost was paid by us and a Finnish welfare group. Subjects were domestic science, gardening, agriculture, animal husbandry. Also handicraft, health and childcare. During their time here, various trips were arranged.

KALEVALA 100 YEARS

Once you get money you want more and hope to have some influence, we were no different. Finland was celebrating the centenary of the Kalevala. The first edition was compiled by Elias Lönnrot and published in 1835 - so the 100th birthday was worth

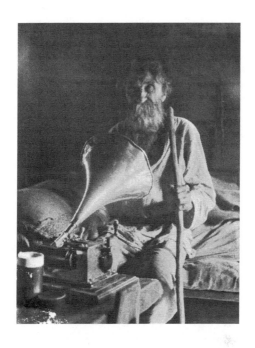

Lauri may have not known that he would marry a lady who is deeply connected with the Kalevala. Anni was directly descended from the younger brother, Triihvo, of Varahvontta Sirkeini/Jamala, who was interviewed by Lönnrot and photographed by Inha.

creating an event. Invitations were sent, and many came to Helsinki from different parts of the world. Arrangements don't always please everybody, I was in that group. Our Association which represented all the Karelian groups around Finland, had no representatives in the front row or even in a corner. Our people were the newest group, and still had a genuine connection to the singing and runes of Viena.

The message from the Finnish nation to Karelian Tribal singers

A hundred years ago Finland stepped forward to the world literature, with the publication of "Kalevala or old Karelian poems depicting the ancient times of Finnish people". It happened with Karelian words and Karelian mood. So this year we send our warmest greetings to Karelia. We thank you for all that Karelia has given us. We also feel very deeply about your destiny.

After the event we had a dispute, which as a hothead I started with an article in the newspapers.

Mikko Karvonen, the editor-in-chief of our paper, calmed the situation by noting that though we were not there, we had the best representation - the KALEVALA. It was all about the importance of this book, and it was present. I was told by a respected, cultured man, "Viena was present". The People were performing, and they were paid, my reply was simple, "We would have sung paid or unpaid". This was not the issue.

Mikko and I remained friends for years, not meeting very often but corresponding regularly kept our friendship going. Sharing ideas about power of people and loathing dictatorship in any form. We were prepared to use tricks to gain the democratic results needed for our own ends, but not in politics. We were idealists, who still hoped for the return of our homeland.

I complained in our paper, but I was not only negative about things. As part of the celebrations, I arranged a publication that I am still pleased with at the age 70, which is now forty years later. *Sanan Mahti* is a large publication. The first half all about Kalevala and second half about the 10th anniversary report of our Central association of the clubs and their work.

I was able arrange meeting with E. N. Setälä. How he felt about the Kalevala. I was able to hammer his words into a granite like form in print - in ink. He was a larger than life person, what were his thoughts and the importance of Kalevala to Karelians. My timing was fortunate, because in the same publication was his obituary; he had died soon after my meeting with him.

I had planned the signatures carefully, inviting the most important in the land: the sitting president Swinhufvud; former presidents K. J. Ståhlberg and L. K. Relander; both archbishops Kaila and Herman; and Marshall Mannerheim.

All good plans can break. The then President Ståhlberg wanted to see the text, but wrote and telephoned informing that he would not sign. Mannerheim, who had been regent in 1918-19, could replace his signature.

An attempt to unite various organisations, failed because of personalities, and their own ambitions. Finally the very old Karjalan Sivistyseura, founded in 1906, and our Central committee decided to work together. At some point Mikko and I had somehow become members. We did not dare to share an office as well, but our paper Itä-Karjala and Karjalan Heimo became one. They were older and more established, so the name Karjalan

Heimo instead of Itä-Karjala was chosen. I enquired "what could happen in case of disagreements. They would have all our advertising clients as well as subscribers?" Their simple answer was - you must not even think about it. Those days will not happen.

Ville Mattinen had become the chairman of KSS. I shared moments in his spacious office in Helsinki, and on one occasion he questioned me. "How do you have the courage to speak. For me money speaks". I replied "Logic". He just nodded.

He is later given a honour - Commercial Councillor. This is granted by the President, but application is made for it by an individual or organisations. A committee of nine chosen for six years will confirm it. So Ville later received one and probably merited it.

Many moments can be left out, some nice and some not. My fears about working together and the paper proved correct. The older society soon showed their mettle, and the publication was taken. Our joint operation stopped, they moved and we were left high and dry. No office, and no paper. We rented a small office near a bird museum, again free like birds in the sky. What now? Standing in the new office, it was a bad time to start a new paper, but somehow an organisation must have a purpose, something to do. Increasing the school side of our work, was most important. The idea that children could live, eat and learn in a school, should work well. The winter was the time for school and in the summer place could be used differently. One could subsidise the other. I remembered my own hungry Christmas, and this could eliminate possible problems that children of refugees have. This gave me an idea for the future.

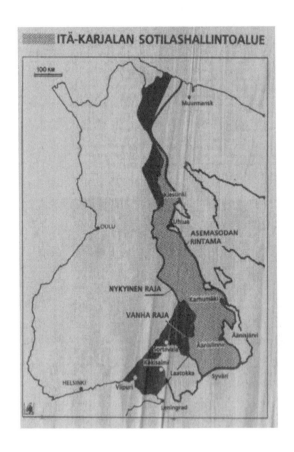

The area under Military Law during the continuation war started 25th June, 1941 and ended 19th September, 1944. Nykyinen Raja is current border. Vanha Raja is the old border.

THE CONTINUATION WAR

I was a Lance Corporal at the start of the Continuation War. Very early one morning a policeman rang the door bell and delivered my orders to report to a meeting. I was sent home for the first night, but next morning woke up to a ringing doorbell again. At the school the Captain felt that the last order is the correct one in the army. I went home again, and after a few days travelled to my first taste of war, ending up in Mikkeli. This was the headquarters of Marshall Mannerheim, who was commander-in-chief. Here I became the secretary to the Advisory Committee's commander. The committee members were made up of the Karelian Freedom Movement leaders. The leadership was elected in Vuokkiniemi[1] 20/7/1941. We shook hands, his was thin, bony and very cold, but a memorable moment for me.

Somebody will talk with me and our group about the future administration of Karelia. This was the land where I was born before escaping to Finland. I took a deep breath. This was a

---

1 *Lauri's second son, Veikko, was born that day in Finland*

moment of change in history that in my earlier dare-devil or reckless speeches, I could never have believed. Yes. While in the club era, the main aim had been to create an educated group of Karelians who could fit into this new life in Finland. Their own country was lost. The loss had now turned into a possibility of regaining their country.

Our new commandant had held high positions in civilian life, and had risen from a lower rank all the way to major and now a lieutenant-colonel in the Army. His adjutant was a lieutenant from the cavalry and as he directed us to a dining room, the spurs made a wonderful noise, which happened frequently during our dinner. Our commandant suggested, advised and gave instructions but said we will not write these down. When we need to talk, we will eat and discuss matters. I believed matters would be well looked after, but when there was need to talk, we ate, the spurs and also our glasses clinked. But nothing was written down.

During the meetings many subjects were talked about. I must mention, that the advisory board did not have power to decide. We put our opinion forward, when asked. We could appeal to the commander-in-chief, although what route we would use was not known to me. Perhaps, if really needed, we could find a way.

The administration and advisory group did not agree on some matters. Such as: religion, local salaries, property, social care, organising educational matters, trade, how to treat the local people and attitudes to Russian people. Perhaps other things as well.

Religion is an example. The administration took the line that the people must change to Lutheranism, but this was not our view. The local people had been raised under the Russian Orthodox religion, and managed to keep their cross whilst under the bolsheviks. We had no right to convert local people. A compromise was achieved - and older people were left in peace but youngsters were registered into the Lutheran doctrine. *(Both Lutheran and The Russian Orthodox churches were more than religions. They were responsible for the registration of all births deaths and marriages, which listed the population.)*

Mannerheim had given orders about salary - people working in the military governed area - were to be paid the same as in Finland, agricultural worker 9 marks per hour and only two marks in Aunus. We had to raise the issue firmly. We had a new commandant who had ordered this poor revision to the local salary, which we disputed.

Property and social matters were difficult, and we managed to discuss but not reach results. People working inside the new military government area were paid, but the sums were noted on their card and they had to repay it eventually. When the bolsheviks arrived in Karelia, the people were told to leave and take their belongings, but we asked them to go and leave everything - they belonged to us. No decision had been made about the collective farms (kolkhoznik). The farms would be kept whole at the moment. They worked for the government (us), so they did not belong to the community.

Culture was a problem. The activities at the theatre at Äänislinna (currently Petroskoi), were not suitable for locals. Our aim was to arrange something not so high brow, which enabled locals to participate also. The Commandant understood and suggested that I talk to a civil servant at his office. I returned to my room and received a phone call from the civil servant who heaped abuse upon me, because I had apparently stepped on his toes.

Trade was another matter - one promised but another would not agree to it. We wanted Karelians to have a share. Some had a shop in Finland and still had one. The aim was to allow some to start a small shop in their home village to help the locals. There was no competition with 'the big boys' who were also wholesalers. We could not see any competition, a promise had been made to us by a fairly senior person, who now had to swallow his promise. Answer was 'NO' and looking back, this was probably good.

The powers that be had already set up Vako as the sole wholesaler and they would set up their own shops. But we had a promise that the local shops already in the hands of Karelians would continue. However, Vako contested this stating that it would bring too much competition, and won.

I had already been involved with the land question in Finland for the refugees who had come to Finland 1918-1920, our committee had a meeting 9/3/1934. This was not an easy issue.

The money. I presented an idea and a good discussion was a base for action. Maybe the government could arrange available land and low interest loans. We printed the forms and distributed amongst the refugee groups. I went with Iivo Härkönen (famous author amongst many things) to present it to Castren at the Ministry of Agriculture, and since he was favourable to it, we prepared the application for the refugees. Iivo and I signed it and presented it on 2/10/1934 to the Ministry, which was not in a hurry. The ministry took their time, "the matter was very difficult, one problem was the obvious - nationality - to own land you had to be Finnish national". Final reply 4/4/1935 was 'No',

The question of land ownership was an issue but this time it was in Karelia, the committee discussed it long and hard. Old/original ownership was not acknowledged, and there was going to be a new sensible way for the future. Local people wanted to open small enterprises like sauna, washing houses, small coffee huts, and fishing which would provide food and money - maybe bartering would take place. Unfortunately nobody seemed know where the nets were 'hiding', result, men remained at home and the fish in the lakes.

Treatment of locals and Russians was apparently the same, but what the reality was I have no knowledge. Some things progressed well as a whole, some differences of course happened.

If I weigh my own part as the secretary, I must admit that perhaps the position at that time was a little difficult, especially as I was gauche and had no military training. There were moments when I was too absolute, if I was right. A freedom fighter is not afraid, when he believes in his course, but there are moments when all must be left for the future to find the solution. It was something I did not yet comprehend, I was not afraid but a courageous servant of my country.

PROMOTION?

At the beginning of the war I was a corporal, it was a long way to gain a promotion and a higher daily allowance. So I was the highest in one level - so were Hitler and Mussolini. Somehow a friend, I have no idea who, mentioned this to somebody. This progressed to a daily order level, but unfortunately the person who was to sign it, saw my name and refused to do so. The daily order was rewritten, and signed in due course, I remained a corporal.

We worked for two and a half years for the Karelians but our views differed from the army's. Their views were so different that finally we decided to bring it to Mannerheim's attention. The result was that the committee was disbanded. It happened quickly and we had no time to put our views. We were not even allowed to have a last meeting. We had to leave our archives for future historians. The commandant informed us that our work would be continued by a newly formed group of local people.

Without explanation and still in uniform I was to go home, but it was not valid in Helsinki, so I was sent back to Viipuri where I stayed the night. This was noted and suddenly I am the highest rank and in charge of soldiers returning from holiday or sick leave. Sleep escaped me that night. Trying to plan how I will hand over the group, what I must do and say. In the morning I met higher ranking officer who passed the responsibility to me. I saluted and growled to the boys "Follow me" and this solved the problem. I passed my command to a sergeant-major, and asked him to return them safely to Äänislinna, the group had a correct ranking officer and I had piece of mind.

As the Continuation War reached its end the number of casualties increased.

Anni had already lost one of her brothers, Jussi, and there remained two brothers. Both were already on the train being made ready to head for the front when they heard their names called out. They stepped off and were given the message sent from the battalion's headquarters: 'Lieutenant Eino Sirkeinen and Lieutenant-Colonel Niilo Sirkeinen are immediately assigned to Mikkeli for duties of the East Karelian military administration'.

At the time, Lauri and Castren were dealing with the establishment of the East Karelian military regime.

Eino wrote "In my opinion, both Castren and Kuntijärvi had their hands in it. I asked the latter years later, and at least he didn't deny it in his vague answer"

The officer who had the earlier problem with my promotion now had a new one. I needed papers to return to civilian life, which took a week. Civilian time was very short - I was sent to Åland, which is group of islands close to Finland. Our purpose was to protect against the Germans, who were now withdrawing from Finland. All the papers were boxed, and people were formed into a military group directed by a staff officer. A new Advisory Committee was not needed.

TRAVELLING WITH NORDSTRÖM

He was a man who was known from the earlier war at the top level in the army. He had fought in 1918, and was great friend of Karelia. At that time he was wounded, and left in the field, but a soldier picked him up, carried him on his back to the first aid station. He just remarked "This man is still breathing" and walked away. A loss of an arm is better than losing your life. Later Nordström found the man and rewarded him.

He arranged his car with a driver to help us during our inspection tours and Mikko and I would travel from village to village in his company, which added importance and humanity to our visit. One place where a sauna was made ready for us, two Russian prisoners were helping with the task. Our commandant insisted that the sauna was shared by all of us. The prisoners were surprised, this was his wish and Mikko and I as lower ranks could not object and did not want to do so.

He was known and welcomed everywhere. During our journey, we stopped at general Talvela's tent for a coffee. He was a commander of the Army Corps. His tent had two rooms, bedroom and second a dining and sitting area. He briefly mentioned the news, we spoke of Karelian prisoners of war. He had six, three of them reconnaissance parachutists, but the other three had been caught wearing uniforms of Finnish army - according to army law he would have to shoot them. The other three he could save. We tried to talk, so few Finnish and Karelian people in the world, but it did not have any effect on the general. We knew him as civilian from earlier encounters before the war, but in here a general is general. We just sipped our coffee and listened.

Our journey continues and there were moments when fear enters you mind - for the colonel it was understandable - he had been wounded in earlier war - but for us as well, fear is suddenly there. On one occasion, we slept in one tent. There had been bombing the night before. On this night, we heard strange noises and a dog barking. I had to go out to see what was happening. The dog had disappeared, and everywhere was calm, so I could reassure everybody all is well.

He was a man who had lost his ships but continued with a shipping agency. Later when asked about his ships. He said "If I need ships again, I will get some" - he was 80.

LIVING QUARTERS

My quarters were situated where the professors lived at university hill. They were not there. I had two rooms and a kitchen, well one room was used by East Karelia Advisory Board, I was in the other room, and the kitchen was sometimes occupied by my brother-in-law Niilo Sirkeinen, who had worked with the finanial papers in Helsinki KKK. He was used to paperwork and money, so he helped us here as well.

Time passed slowly as a war at this time. I travelled to Finland, looked after KKK matters, newspapers and somehow there was still time for stories. So I decided to write a book 'Yhdessä Ylenivät'. A story that combined three tribal wars. The background was Karelian village life, three families and army people.

I managed to finish it and Werner Söderström (WSOY) was the publisher. A reputable company, also Haavio gave a good review, suggesting that even he would be happy to put his name as the author. The book had both positive reviews and criticism. It was felt that I should have expanded it. The third family was hurt by events, but I had mentioned it in passing and the critic did not notice. Well, he did not see it and a critic is always correct!

I was also right, because I gained reputation as a writer, and money. The print was 8000 and sold out on pre-orders. I became a wealthy man.

A windfall! 8000 soft back copies at 65 marks each totals 520,000

MY SPEECH 23/8/1942 - ÄÄNISLINNA

"We have celebrated this tribal festival in Finland with various themes but this is the first time in our Karelian capital. The emotional feeling of standing on our land and shaking the hand of our own people is more than you can imagine.

This is how we started our life in Finland. In a few years, from this group of people, arose a variety of work - sawmills, factories, some started their own shops and so on. Schools opened their doors to many children. Old people who had come over, were given help with 'board and lodgings' - retired people were given shelter in the eve of their lives. We all tried to arrange our own life, and next viewed people and life around us.

We could see a young Finnish state, young but a well educated nation. We could see an industrious, persistent people, who have ideas and ideals, moving forward, and making tomorrow a better day than the day before.

As we became familiar with ways of the country, we became attached and closer to it - and started to regard it as our own. Still there was something inside us which reminded us of you here. We must not forget where we have come, in our mind there are no borders in a country.

We came from here, and this could be seen in many ways in Finland, what we wrote in newspapers, music and cultural events, our flag. We met each other in the festivals like today. During these times we could relive our childhood times and remember all of you here. We received letters from the mines of Ural regions, which informed us of you. You know the history of the letter writer better than we in Finland. I mention it, so that you know that we were aware, but could not offer a helping hand.

Finnish people also wanted to help, but neither could do so. We created Karelian focused clubs, which sole purpose was to help and educate. This is the first time here, but like a good companion, it has come here too.

We have returned.

RAGNAR NORDSTRÖM

from Wikipedia

After the outbreak of the Winter War, Ragnar Nordström acquired weapons for the field army. As a condition for the transfer of armaments to the Defense Forces, he made it necessary that the armaments be used to strengthen the Lapland front. The weapons he bought, including artillery, were of great importance in stopping the enemy's attack on the northern front. After that, he guaranteed arms sales in Finland and Germany and participated in the costs of a Finnish SS battalion sent to the eastern front, although he had initially opposed the creation of the entire troop unit. After Finland took over the war in East Karelia, Ragnar Nordström invested in the schooling of Karelian children in the territory.

This man was very important - to Finland, and to Lauri.

Below is an interview with his son at a reunion of the school in Loviisa.

"As you will read, when Finland occupied Karelia during the Continuation War June 1941- September 44, Lauri was part of an advisory committee giving advice to the military government ruling the occupied territory. He found that the population were either of Russian or Karelian stock. Mindful of his own escape to Finland, he tried to help some of the Karelian children. He joined with Nordström, and together they started at least two Kotitalo's - homes for orphaned and refugee children. Located close to and associated with a normal day school, these homes gave bed and board to the displaced children. Lauri recognised the need, and implemented the idea using Nordström's money. Lauri, who was based in Äänislinna (now named Petroskoi) - the capital of the occupied territory - was in the perfect position to find the children in need, and with his frequent trips to Helsinki, saw that things ran smoothly at the home.

Kaarina and I had learned that there was to be a school reunion at one of these schools. The organiser was Nordström's son, Martti-Ragnar, and on the chosen August weekend, we found ourselves in Loviisa, a charming small town about 100 miles along the coast from Helsinki towards the Russian border. The original school had been started by Nordström senior, and his son was present at the reunion. The boarding school that was instigated by Lauri was represented by his daughter, Kaarina. The children of the two founders met for the first time. Martti-Ragnar. is a charming man, wiry and fit with masses of energy that belies his 70 odd years. It was only after the formal day's speeches and dinner before he was able to take some time to himself, and the following story fell from his lips - casually as though the story of which he spoke was normal.

In 1939 - November 27th, the Russians opened fire and invaded Finland. The two countries had been in negotiation for

Air-raid damage in Helsinki, date November 30th, 1939

months. Russia wanted to annex Finland, to impose its own socialist regimes in exchange for strategic land and islands. This was to safeguard Russia's second city, Leningrad, which was uncomfortably close to the edge of Russian territory, and at the head of an narrow stretch of water. Russia controlled one side of this, but Finland the other.

The Russian high command wanted a quick answer, and opened the attack on four fronts along 800 miles. They threw in 600,000 troops, with 1,700 tanks. They had 3000 bombers and fighters. etc. To meet this onslaught, Finland had just 250,000 men, 13 tanks, 100 anti tank weapons, 160 antiquated bi-planes and Fokkers. During the preceding months, when war looked inevitable, the Finns were called to arms. But they were pitifully equipped, lacking uniforms, rifles, machine guns etc..

Looking at a photo of Nordström, I saw at once that he had an empty sleeve. "That happened in the first world war", Martti-Ragnar explained. "You must have been a big boy during this period?". "Yes, I was around eleven or twelve. I was used to following my father around wherever he went. I was his 'right arm', you see. He could not dress properly without assistance and had difficulty with the calf length riding boots, sam brown etc. I used to travel with him in the car or by train, and stayed outside the meetings. I learnt a great deal about slot machines. In one hotel, the staff were ordered to keep me in change, so that I could spend the day playing on the machines until his meeting ended.

"I remember one day. We had gone to Helsinki to the War Office. Father was inside asking Marshall Mannerheim if he would place all of the war effort for the North of Finland under his control. As I stood on the street, the bombing started. It was

the day that the war broke out, and I could see the bombs dropping, hear the explosions, and see the fires starting.

When we had returned north to our farm by train, there was a phone call from the commanding officer of all the northern Finnish forces. "Nordström, can you help? I have at least 2,000 men armed with only their puukko knives, and wearing a band round their civilian clothes by way of uniform. And I have the Russian 14th army on my door step!!".

Nordström telephoned his agents in Sweden. "Can you get me rifles and ammunition? machine guns?".They were to look into it, but it would require a personal visit. Phoning the nearest railway station, he spoke to the station master. "When is the next train to Sweden?" "In about 5 minutes, Sir" "Hold it. I'll come at once".The train was held while he packed and crossed 70 kilometres of Northern Finnish roads.

When he arrived at Stockholm, he was told that the sale of the guns was not going to be easy. Firstly, Sweden was neutral, and it would require the authority of the Swedish parliament to permit their release to Finland. Secondly, how are they to be paid for? Did Nordström have the authority of the Finnish Government for such a purchase? when would the cash be available? Here at least was a stroke of luck - if the loss of two ships can be called luck. Nordström's Swedish bank had just received the payout for two total loss claims from his insurance underwriters. He gave his word that he would guarantee payment from his own personal funds already in a Stockholm bank, and "When can parliament reconvene?" How was not told, but he was able to arrange a special plenary session of the Swedish parliament - who approved the sale of the weapons.

The sale was approved on December the 5th. By the 10th, they were in the hands of the front-line soldiers.Within one hour, sev-

eral Russian tanks had been destroyed. The Russians never broke through the northern front. No one who studies an account of this Winter War can be in any doubt that those weapons played a significant role. And sitting opposite me telling this detail of history, was the 'boy' who pulled up his dad's boots, and who had stood outside the Finnish War Office, watching the first bombs rain down on the defenceless population.

But there is a postscript, and because one of the supporting characters in the story is the Soviet Union, this postscript has a chilling centre.

The actual school had been in place for a number of years already, started by Nordström senior to educate the local children. This school continued uninterrupted to the present day, and all but three of the 100 plus attendees to the reunion where made up of generations of the local children. It is now the local senior high, and will last for many decades into the next century.

However, the kotitalo - the home house - where the orphaned or refugee children where nurtured, lasted only until the end of the war when peace was signed. I presume that new children could not cross over the border to replenish the older ones as they left. But also, any institution, magazine, society etc. that had connections with Karelia (the occupied territory now retaken by the USSR) was strictly forbidden by the terms of the peace agreement. Because of the activity of the Finnish and Soviet secret police, any person associated with such activities was in a very dangerous position. Thus the school benefited only the 50 pupils, and for just the duration of the Continuation War. Lauri's position close to the centre of the administration controlling the occupied territory, helped him to discover children who were prime candidates for the school. I don't recall the figures exactly now, but the first intake had around 50 children, the vast *majority of whom had Lauri's hand in there somewhere to help their application and approval, travel documents and permissions, etc.*

"But, of these children, only seven survive" continued Martti-Ragnar. "When the Russians made their final offensive to recapture the territory, it was summer time and many of the children had returned to Petroskoi, to friends or family. Once the push gathered momentum and the land recaptured by the Russians, they were stranded back behind the lines, and unable to return to the school. Those who were caught by the Soviet authorities and admitted that they had been in Finland were tried and sentenced to imprisonment in Siberia. If the child held the secret, then they were not taken, surviving to lead a normal life. But whenever they admitted their days in Finland, then they were punished Soviet style. Of course, some did not survive the Siberian conditions, and these sentences were the cause of many deaths. Five years in a gulag for going to school in Finland!".

We met Martti-Ragnar the next morning for breakfast, and he brought with him a copy of a manuscript that had been written by one of the pupils in the last year or two. Now close to his eighties and in ill health, he had been unable to travel to Finland. He was to have been the sole representative of the former pupils who had returned and lived in Russia. He was one of the children who had kept the secret. It was only three years ago that he had confessed his past to his wife, and with the help and encouragement from Martti-Ragnar had put his story down on paper."

Notes from an interview of Martti-Ragnar Nordström by David Worsley - August, 2000.

HOW TO ARRANGE CIVILIAN LIFE

The end of the war various permits were needed. Earlier, a refugee needed permission from the governor of the county to remain there. At first they were for six months, but in 1924 they became annual. Moving from one area to another also required permission. A work permit from Home Office meant problems in many ways. Those without nationality could only own land and property with a special permit. The tax deductions were different, and counties tried to avoid social immigrants because of costs of hospitals, schooling etc.

It was possible to apply for it, but expensive and the county needed to give a report, often a negative one. Why, because the county feared, that a large family would stay and drain the resources.

I had a residence permit for a foreigner, I am married have wife and two children and third is due in the summer. I have been in Finland since 1922. It was my turn to apply for Finnish nationality. The end of war means a beginning of new life, because my

83

work with East Karelian Advisory Board and as secretary of KKK ended. All the happenings to do with the demands in the armistice and anything to do with Karelia was no longer allowed.

My first identity paper was one given by an official at Kemi. My name is still Kundozeroff and date of birth was 20/4/1909, this was a permit of residence. As a secretary of KKK I had helped many with the paperwork and money to apply for their nationality. Now it was my turn. I had help, because to search for your time in Finland required in my case 30 documents, which required money. You have to trace your movement in the country - two Orthodox church papers, one Medical paper, five Tax office papers, five State police papers, one Criminal police paper, three Reports from the Helsinki police, and recommendations from three people. I believe my paper mountain was bigger than the ones I handled for the refugees.

My old professor Lauri Kettunen wrote a letter confirming my ability to use the language and support my family. The papers gathered and were finally submitted by November 14 1944 (Kaarina[1] is now almost 3 months old). The bundle was submitted by proxy, because I was now in hiding in the deepest Finland. The place was remote, no electricity. There was no post box and it had to be collected a few kilometres away.

I had bought a farm on the November 28th, 1944 with a friend's help, something I could not do alone. I saw a newspaper advert, "A farm for sale", that has been empty for a long time. I must find the money for this.

Many people left the country after the war for fear of either prosecution or being returned to Russia. I wanted to remain in

---

1 *She was christened Sisko Kaarina - but as she grew older, the family called her Kaarina*

> CERTIFICATE BY Professor Kettunen
>
> I hereby certify that, I knew Mr Lauri Kuntijärvi during 1938-46, when the undersigned was chairman of the Support Association for Väinölä school. He was the secretary, and achieved koulukoti status for the school, where refugee children could live whilst studying in the local school. He was also my student at Civic College at Helsinki (founded 1925). He already showed great fluency in writing and was a very talented speaker.
>
> Pakila 7/1/1946 Professor Kettunen

Finland but had to disappear for a while for the same reasons. I was not a Finnish national.

The post brings a letter. I open it, it is very large, inside is a Savings bank book and a letter. The book contains - 2,000 marks. This is the final amount for my war time service - the balance of five years. With Tyynelä and me (as my children's guardian) I purchased the house and farm, which had 2,5 hectare cultivated land, 4,5 arable, but marsh or fenland, 3 hectares of forestry. This included buildings as well.

THE ROMANCE OF COUNTRY LIFE

Now I am going to be a farmer. I have kept my flat in Helsinki, just in case. We can sell all the unnecessary items, like the radio - there is no electricity - I can also make our furniture. We finally arrive, last part on a horse and carriage, and the road is getting smaller and smaller. Log cabin, cowshed, woodsheds and sauna appear in the middle of the forest. We check the rooms, but the important thing is to light the range to cook food for the children.

My plantation

Three children, Heimo Antero 4, Veikko Olavi 3 and Sisko Kaarina is only 3 months.

We must unload and get everything inside. Finding firewood was a little harder, there was a well, but where can we eat? we left table and chairs in Helsinki.

Anni laughs, I had promised to make them, so I just replied 'You wait'. We have a grand picnic on the floor and everything is good when you are hungry. The cabin needed cleaning, so many steps were needed before our bed was ready. The cart unloaded, borrowed horse sheltered, enough wood carried in for the night, end result was a bed on the floorboards. Children first, then Annikki, who was here to help with the children, then Anni my wife and last myself stretched on our communal bed.

My plantation was 10 hectares, of which 3 was cultivated, as a man who wanted have order not chaos in my new life, I made a list of work. In spring it all looked so promising and almost romantic. My plan was not so good, idea was to spread small amount of manure from the cowshed on field in front of a window. Sow wheat and when the time was right I could stand in front of this field - take photos and have someone take them as I inspected my harvest. It would be up to my chest, I am not very tall, so it is not difficult. We can all dream. The photo I had planned carefully was a disaster. The manure helped the growth, but the first downpour flattened it and it stayed down, so I could not play the part of the proud farmer in front of his harvest.

Before giving up my farming life, I tried chicken farming. My neighbour and I decided to buy chickens, 100 each, I left mine to the professionals, incubator would do the work and deliver me little chicks later. Neighbour had just bought a feed boiler and wanted to save the cost. Many of us had doubts about his method.

Result - 60 chickens and 40 cockerels = 100, he had 100 burnt eggs.

ANNI's LETTERS

Anni was working in Helsinki and could only take a holiday to visit the family. Sisko Kaarina was in town with her most of the time. We have seven letters that she wrote from Helsinki from 1/2./1946 to 5/5/1946.

Dear Hubby,   Helsinki 1/2/1946

I am writing but I have not heard from you for a long time. Did you get the parcel? What did Antero say about his new shoes? Hope they are the right size. I was afraid that, Veikko's feet would suffer because his shoes are so small. Boys must be spending a lot of time outside, what about weather there, snow and is it freezing? We have lots snow and temperatures -10 to -15 every day, writing this at lunch, did not want to go out. My position is now permanent, looking after all the accounts of the bookshops, much better than before, and I have an assistant. Asked about holiday, but did not ask for an increase in salary, pity. Current holiday is 4 weeks, and by summer have been here for 10 years so I will have a whole month. This year there is also a winter holiday - if I take 3 days from summer break, it will give me a week as a winter break. I have asked for a break at Easter, which would give me 8 days. This is the longest we have been apart. You can't come here. Boys are waiting for summer, tell them

An extract from a letter to Eino, my brother-in-law 4/10/45

We are relatively well. The boys have been lifting carrots. Next week is threshing, which will take only 3-4 hours, and I will see results of our year. As I said earlier, potato harvest was magnificent. Also berries and mushrooms are plentiful and we pick them. The ram is destined for the pot soon. So the pot will bubble and give us tasty meals.

Antero was 5 years old and Veikko 4

that mum and Sisko will come before summer. Many nights still to sleep until we see you. Sisko has had stomach problem and has been in hospital for 3 weeks. I visited her, but it was very difficult for both us. Will try to telephone, and go and see the consultant, what is the problem? She will have to stay here until I come there next.

Have you received the magazines, 3 for you and one for the boys, if not let me know.

I brew a coffee at home, lunch at the office and I go to mother for evening meal - it has worked very well so far.

The artists are staying here until end of February, my brother Eino, is staying at mums and Irene at her mum. Cannot arrange anything else, because rent tribunal people have asked about him. Where is he living? Maybe they will arrange a place for him, we are aware of problems here. When 'FRIENDS' are getting large apartments by miracle arrangements, and the person living in the flat are just asked to leave. I don't want get involved in anything.

War criminal cases seem to be delayed by a phone call from an important person, there was a meeting where a life sentence was demanded. It will not happen, it is political.

Next week there is a birthday party, Risto Sirkeinen will be 50, everybody will come. Asked if somebody could bring a few eggs, which I will return when our chickens will lay. Eggs are 40-50 marks here, also butter, and milk would be

Sisko Kaarina at 'the Plantation'

good. I could bake something for Sisko, I am sure she will get well again. Maybe you can get milk from neighbours without coupons, so I can use the coupons here. This month five days milk was allowed against children's coupons. A month and another calf will be added to our livestock, so life will ease a little. Two cows and a calf, but who is to do the milking now?

Have you been able to write? How is the shop going? Send the papers to Ida, I am sure she can send you something. Some papers will be needed, but try your luck anyway. Just for the cost of the stamp, so it makes sense. One of the Väinölä boys has been diagnosed with an ulcer, and he is due to take exams. Doctor ordered a bed rest for a month, he is so unhappy, in case he'll miss his exams. He can sit them a month later, so that is good. Lunch over 15 minutes ago, return to work. I will send you 3000 marks, more at the beginning of the month.

Give a kiss to boys and yourself from me and Sisko. Write a long letter about the boys activities, it is nice read - I can almost see them. Regards to Liisa. If she can send her clothing coupon, I will try to get her stockings, and for the boys the extensions for their socks. Useful in the winter.

In haste but with lots of love Anni

Dearest Lasse   Helsinki 3/2/46

Why don't you write? Are you still ill or what is wrong? I have been away for 3 weeks and not a line from you. Two ordinary letters and two registered letters, which had the coupons. I have also telephoned the neighbour to find out. I am very worried about everything, food in particular. I have asked Ida (her sister, who lives in Vaasa) to send some meat, it should be there soon. How is the pig growing - will it provide food soon and the cows, still getting milk, and the chickens. Here shops are full of eggs, price varying from 25 - 19.50 per egg. Downward trend in price, how could you send us some? Here is a list of everything I would like to have from there. Onions are 86 marks per kilo, if you can send I don't have buy here. I would like have the small coffee pot, and a bed cover, you can use a blanket as a cover, sheets will keep clean longer that way. I have still been eating at mums but sleep here at home. When the artist friends leave, I will start to cook at home, I have booked a cleaner because if all goes well at the rent tribunal in May, they will leave. He asked me to evict them so that they can get a place of their own. I am not happy, hope we will not get into trouble over this.

Can you send me the tax papers? What are we doing with cottage, file papers here or there and I also need your tax information. Advance taxes are being sent. Shall I send you the money or bank it here?

Do boys remember us two at all? I asked Sisko about Antero and Veikko where are they, her reply was boys. She was searching for the cat in every corner of the room and when gran showed a car and man out of the window, her reply was dad. Of course it was not, you are there. Now she is back in hospital again, crying all the time. Mother suggested that I should not go, until she settles more.

How is the shop working? Have you asked Lammela about permission to have one? What about Ida, written to her yet? It is Sunday and I am working overtime. Next week will send you a small parcel, as soon as you get the card, collect it from the post office.

Cheese is available next week, so will send some as a taster and also herrings. I can send some, if you cannot get them. And butter, are you able churn any? You can also ask our neighbour for more milk (I know they are far) and if any butter is on offer, please accept. I can easily place it here. I am still eating at mums, but soon start to cook here. Must work overtime, last quarter is not done yet and it is already February. I look forward to a nice long letter soon, will not write until I get one from you with news.

All my love to boys and you. I could really do with a nice long letter from you. Regards to Liisa and ask her to look after the three children there.

Best wishes and good night Anni

Dear Lasse   Helsinki 9/2/46

Thank you for your long awaited letter which finally arrived here. I am relieved to hear that your illness was not as serious as I was told. I am worried about boys' shoes, if they are too small and it is cold, you cannot put a second sock. I will try send a new pair for Antero and Veikko can have his, so two pairs of socks will fit. Sock situation is not very good, if I can get some wool, maybe Liisa could knit some. Sisko needs new socks also. I sent you a pair, did they arrive? Niilo (Anni's brother) managed to get new woollens for boys. The leggings will be done soon, maybe you can sow a piece from an old blanket to make the top of the boot stronger.

You both must be very busy to forget that all the washing is drying in the loft. The large cardboard box has the dirty laundry and clean sheets are drying in the loft. Try to change the sheets sometime, clean sheets will make you feel better.

I visited Sisko in hospital, had a little cake for her. She ate it, even the small pieces from the blanket. She happily played and laughed, but as soon as I left, she started crying again. I will go again on Sunday and with cake in my bag. A lady visiting a person in next bed, was mummy, or she called her mummy. She also asked for a cake. I don't know what happens, when she comes home. Siiri is also in hospital, but maybe she can help later.

I need the tax book, it is asked at the office. If you have nothing else to write, just send the book, although I would really like to hear about all of you. We have had terrible snow storms for 3 days, and it is really cold. Do you have snow there?

Have you noticed from the papers that Rahikainen[1] has died 2/2 and funeral is 17/2. Rinne telephoned and sent a message to you. He really wants you to come and speak at the funeral. All I could say, how it is. It is probably not possible, but you will be thinking on the day.

The taxes about the cottage, we need to do it in both places - here and there using form B. Have you done anything, I will do my part here. Also the rent tribunal, it was disallowed. I was so cross that I could scream. Will send the parcel registered mail, hope you are all keeping well.

With love Anni

Dear Lasse   Helsinki 4/3/46

Thanks for your letter. I am not in the mood but will try to pen a few words. Feeling really low. Last Friday I happily brought Sisko home. It was good to have her home again. I

---

1 *Rahikainen was the chairman of the East Karelian Advisory Board, appointed by Mannerheim.*

noticed she was not right, terrible cough and irritable. Sunday she was not hungry and she could not swallow, by evening her temperature rose to 39.3. Monday morning I had to phone the doctor, who diagnosed tonsillitis and she is back in hospital. I could not look after her at home, I have workload for two people, somebody is on holiday. I was going to just take next week off and come to you in the country, but all fell through with her illness.

I got your letter in the morning and really missed you all, then taking Sisko to hospital again, but your phone call should have made me feel better. Your voice and choice of words made me think it was my fault that she is in hospital again. You did not mean it, but feeling emotional was my problem not yours. Boys' overalls need replacing, so all I could do was to cry my eyes out. I have not done the overalls yet, because I am working until nine o'clock every night, I am sure you are asleep over there. So it is not Helsinki, which is enchanting me as you wrote, a reality is we need the money. I have collected bits and pieces and will send a parcel soon.

I am too tired to answer your letter now. It was so good to have the letters from boys. I will get the overalls done somehow next week. If you can come next week, can we talk about what you wrote. Would be good to see the boys and they would like it too. How will you manage if Sisko will be there as well, to manage three is hard. Maybe Liisa could look after the boys there if you come alone. I cannot say what is best, brain says one thing and emotions an other. Loving kisses and good night. See you soon - your sad Anni

PS Have you ordered the coffee? If not, do so, it is always best to use the coupons.

PS Can the boys use the shirts I am sending now, and save the new ones. Veikko's shirt is red and Antero blue one.

Dear Lasse   Helsinki 24/4/46

Thanks for everything. I am back, but it was really hard. Train journey was awful. Car not so bad, sat in the front, but next stop 4 more people at Hinnerjoki. At the front 3 ladies and a child plus the driver. Also two men on top of the load. Next is Peräpohja, where I was in the cabin travelling to Pori, could sit for a moment only, all seats were sold. So rest was just hanging on somehow, feeling really sick and headache did not help. Went to mum from the station, had something to eat and got home at 9 o'clock. The young couple had returned, but not at home at the moment. Went to bed at ten and woke up 7.15. So feel good today. What did children say in the morning, when mum had disappeared? Antero unhappy because he could not come? and little Sisko? Veikko of course took everything calmly. Do tell me quickly how everything progresses? I will go and collect my luggage with my brother Niilo. Let you know what happens. You can send more flour, already sold what I had for 100 marks per kilo. Writing this at work, want to post it and you will get it by Saturday. Regards to all of you and to Liisa and Mikko. Bye and with my love Anni

H:ki 29/4/46

Heat does not break your bones, but this cold will certainly do so. Cottage there, must be nice and warm. We had thunder and lightning and rain here yesterday - not long but really powerful and noisy. On the radio there was a talk about the delegation's trip to Moscow, some were clapping for what? Have you arranged the pig affair, the sooner the better, as the weather gets warmer it will could get little risky. I have arranged the 'delivery', and hope it will be satisfactory. Sorry about 'Esko's signature (a tear has fallen on the ink and blotched the letter, the large ink mark is called Esko-'mark).

I will send you all the money that I have managed to collect so far. How are the children getting on? Is Liisa managing to arrange clean clothes and food for all of you? (Radio had a programme about East Karelia and stolen properties and then the folks clapped, why?) Life is really strange now.

I am worried about all of you, but particularly about the little one, she is so dependant on everybody and everything. Has the snow gone and weather getting better so that she can spend time outside? Does she remember me or has already forgotten me.

Family news, Eikka, my brother also called Eino, had a son last Sunday at 11.50 and 3.5 kg is good weight. I am so sad for him, we had at least a place to live when Antero was born, but they have to live in two places. He will be in Kokkola, to do some research for an airport. Whilst he is there Irene will be with her mother, nice to have company. When he returns what then?

Did you get anybody to do the ploughing? And what about the head farm hand (foreman - you) working well? Chickens laying any eggs, perhaps you could send some here. They are 25 marks now, but when I came the price was eye watering 650 marks a kilo.

All of you are asleep, it is 23.00 and I am also tired. Kisses, take care. Anni

PS. Flour and meat 3000 marks, and 500 for Liisa's salary, I left you 1000. I went to pay the insurance for Veikko, and nearly passed out. It was 880, so can't send any more now. I think you should not talk about the milk coupons, we have not said anything before and it could cause a problem. Maybe leaving it will be a better option.

Helsinki 5/5/46

Dear Lasse

Thank you for your simple perhaps even modest letter! Contents only, hello and goodbye. I am crying silently, missing you all so much. It is so lonely. How are the boys and Sisko? Is it dry and warm so that she can be outside, boys can cope, but she is so tiny. I was not so lonely, when she was here. Are the fields black? You cannot plant yet. I heard that the real country folk do not sprout potatoes, result - no blight on potatoes. Perhaps they know from experience, and you can do the same. Is the grass green? We have a little. One more month and the cows can go out, it will be easier for Liisa, but there will more work from somewhere else.

Is Mikko still enthusiastic or is it waning? Write a little more, you were very sparse with your words.

Mayday came and went. Students marched, and the eve of Mayday places were full of paper flowers and balloons. Expensive if you bought a balloon, prices between 100 - 1000 marks. I went to Siiri. How did you celebrate the day over there? I enclose a demand from the tax office. They do not forget, it is from 1942, also you have to produce your military passport. I am sure it was paid, but how can be find old receipt in this chaos, so we must pay. Tell me what you think, must pay by 16.5. I will send a parcel at the same time. Share the contents with the girls, who help.

It was Antero's birthday, he was 6 years old and we both forgot. I will send some goodies, so that you can have a party now. - I managed to get some lye for the soap making. It is very runny, trying to find out how to send it. Perhaps Lammela, the shop, would have some, and you could exchange it for a soap coupon.

I have not heard about the pig sale here, you should place the rest of the pig soon. Weather is getting warmer and it could spoil.

Have not got the cloth for our artist's girl. The wedding is soon.

You all are asleep but I must sleep here alone. Be well and give my love to children in the morning. Anni

PS Have you remembered to give Sisko cod liver oil? Send me the tax paper back. Tuulikki's books cost 150 marks. Payment in eggs please.

WRITING IS BETTER THAN FARMINg

I returned to Helsinki. I had sold the farm to an immigrant family, who was to pay by government bonds. This took a year, but she was so unhappy about losing the interest on them that I agreed to a payment in paper money, I also agreed to her keeping the government bonds. I lost a lot, but my soul felt good, maybe her need was greater than mine[1]. With my depleted funds I purchased - in my wife's name - a small plot of land in Rekola, it had a one room cottage with an attic. It was Christmas time when the chickens arrived by train. They stayed at Helsinki station for a while and the staff collected the eggs for their own use. Eggs were still rationed, so it was like a present, a Christmas present.

The automatic chicken coop worked well for years in this new place close to Helsinki. They were in a shed which was warmed with large lights and floor made of turf to keep them warm, also unlimited food. I went three times a week to collect the eggs, and had variety of customers, probably without coupons, who were

---

1 *This generous gesture is a measure of his philosophy*

*"A very inquisitive, talkative but deep thinking man.
He is the owner and editor-in-chief of a bureau called Keskustalehtien Uutistoimisto.*

A journalist is part of democracy who will keep people informed of the politicians. He is a servant of the country who tells how the elected representatives manage the country's affairs.

*He is not bound by party politics and can freely write, because the next election is not important to him personally."
(Kuvaposti 4 - 27/10/60)*

happy to have the eggs. Chickens lived a long time, years it seemed. Life improved, maybe the need for my enterprise was no longer necessary. So the end of chickens, or the manure really, spelt the end of good harvest on my plot, where we grew vegetables, strawberries, various currants. Maybe I will start to use this new biodynamic gardening.

My chicken farming was not going to support the family, so I must find work - anything. Looking at adverts I noticed a vacancy for a news reader - dictating other people's work. It was part time, in the evening, and reading somebody's words, I did not like it much, but forced myself to do it. Hourly wage, low, but I was in the right atmosphere again, politics and new people. Soon a new reporter was needed, I offered and wrote samples of my work. My first day with a professional routine did 18 articles on various subjects. I was offered a position, but the head Möller, laughingly suggested that this speed will soon cause problems. They will sack everybody and leave just one to do the work. In my defence I was able say the following "when it is your work, you write and eventually my sources will run dry". This will also happen to me. He was an amusing man, from Denmark. Danish is not a language, it is like a sore throat, that is why he had learned other languages.

A working journalist mentioned that "Yes I-am working now as a journalist, but I am planning not just to tell but also to do things", he eventually became the prime minister of Finland. Soon I became aware, that I was now inside the political world. Before the war I had studied administrative law and journalism. As a member of the Advisory Committee during the Continuation War my task was to observe and report. Now I am doing both - observing and writing.

My personality could not vote for a person who would only observe their own interest into government. So looking inside political life made me aware - it was not for me. Imagine three highly regarded people getting ready for government meeting, with a sole purpose grinding the opposition down. They were from this country, trying to keep country going well, but their main purpose was to gain power and to remain there.

I was often in their meetings and received praise. Talking about the sources of the news, I mentioned the following "You talk about the little things, not big ones. The field is like the sea, small fishes are at surface, but the big ones are deeper. You must expose big ones which swim deep. . . . . ". My words were remembered, but nobody revealed the big fish. Editors had to find the 'fish' themselves. Only if the politician wants to reveal this for his own benefit, will it be revealed.

My source mentioned once the land ownership of various politicians. One had a zero hectares and he did not like it when it was published. I survived the story, but an other one caused a problem. The murder of Sdanov was blamed on Stalin by our correspondent in Sweden, I was working in the evening and had no censorship instructions. So the story was published. The correspondent lost his job in Sweden, I survived, but left sometime later. Reason? Don't know, I was regarded as a talented journalist, but would not join the union, whose members wanted positions. My final salary was not correct, they did not pay my holiday money. I argued with the owner: "You were involved with making laws for holidays as well as holiday money. There are always consequences for our actions, I expect the money to be paid, or "I will see you in court". I was paid, and our friendship remained intact.

I was an unemployed sergeant again, but had capital from the book, but not enough interest to live on. I left the farm, the chicken enterprise is finished and I have lost this last work. I was a known figure after the war, but I needed work now. Various political parties had their own papers, but there was a gap. The liberals had four wealthy and a few smaller non party ones but did not have a bureau. So I founded a bureau to serve as their news provider in Helsinki at the Houses of Parliament. I had my permanent pass to the House. I was interviewed and had very favourable reports about my work, such luck. However my office had some weaknesses. The newspapers were the best in their location and expected a very good service from me. I was the weakest in terms of number of reporters, I was the only one. The other political parties supported many papers with their funds, and obviously had large budgets. Mine was not in the same class, so I had to work harder and sometimes felt it in my shoulders.

My bureau lasted for fourteen years. Observing all the party members was a revelation, when a person is talking in the parliament to empty walls, the audience being only the speaker of the house and a person recording, it is hard to understand why they do it. An event in their home town would be cancelled, but here in the parliament they speak with enthusiasm, and the real thing is making laws and politics.

The law must be applied to everybody equally, but when a politician is in front of the judge, the result can be interesting. Maybe it was lack of judgement or no knowledge of the matter, and when this was the basis of the judgement, there was a vague smile on the accused's face, and small fine would complete the case. He would most likely return to his seat at the parliament.

A small event took place when the country had high ranking visitors from next door. During the visit the pair, our president and a herd of journalists wandered around Helsinki, and further afield to countryside. A nice farm was the destination, and was prepared for our visit, rooms had nice light coloured carpets which we all muddied well and truly. Everything went well until we visited a sauna building. The president is a very tall man, but the door frame was low. This resulted in an accident and the president's head was damaged. I was next to him, and enquired "What now?" His reply "When you have reached a very high position in life, you may think that you have no need to bow to anybody, and then a doorframe teaches you a lesson." I queried "A lesson is always good, but how is the head? Is it still needed?" The Russian visitors travelled with a doctor, who patched his head with a plaster.

Earlier in life we have all written irresponsibly, and later it may or may not surface and damage the person. In Finland the election of the president was a healthy competition between the candidates. Our normal election system changed. In my own work, it was necessary to know the core of the politics, this was possible by wandering around the corridors and corners, where you could hear who could decide, who was just fodder and not important at all. Here you could perhaps find the fish in the deep sea, as I have suggested earlier, and get a story for your paper.

An issue, the introduction of comprehensive school, was important to me in particular as I had spent perhaps a third of my life's work in helping to educate the refugees from Karelia. There are ways to bring in a new system, almost like smuggling, by testing this new model in the North as well as other parts of Finland. Whilst at same time passing a different resolution in the parliament. In this instance, there was a report about the new schools which did not include any costs. The author said "Culture is priceless. When you need the money, you just take".

I was livid about this way of thinking, but somehow had to admire the clever and scheming way they achieved it. Maybe this system would help, because the primary schools were loosing their brightest pupils, who would take a baccalaureate and go to university, now they could keep a mixture of pupils.

LEINO - COMMUNIST - HOME OFFICE

During the Winter War Leino stayed underground, hiding in communist safe-houses across the Finnish countryside. In those years, Leino became acquainted with his future wife Hertta Kuusinen. In 1940, Leino was detained in a secure facility. His detention continued until 1941, when he escaped from a prison train in Riihimäki, which was taking prisoners to fight in a penal battalion. Leino participated in underground Communist Party activities until the 1944 armistice between Finland and the Soviet Union and the legalization of the Communist Party.

In the 1945 parliamentary elections, Leino was elected Member of Parliament for the Finnish People's Democratic League (SKDL) from Kuopio. Leino remained in parliament until 1950. He became Minister at the Home Office in 1945. Leino's time at the Home Office is often referred to as Finland's "years of peril", as the far left control over the Home Office and therefore the internal security apparatus of the nation raised fears of a communist takeover.

In the spring of 1948, Leino was the SKDL representative in the delegation which negotiated the Finno-Soviet YYA treaty in Moscow. Some days before the delegation's departure to Moscow,

Leino met with the Chief of Defence, General Aarne Sihvo, and presented him with concerns about extreme right-wing and left-wing demonstrations that suggested a coup. Leino asked that the army secure order in Finland while the YYA[1] was being negotiated.

President Paasikivi released Leino from his duties at the Home Office in 1948. Parliament had adopted a motion of censure of Leino with connection to his illegal handing over of nineteen people to the Soviet Union in 1945.

I was told the following by Minister Vesterinen.

"Leino was a lonely man who did a great service to his country. A few days before a planned rebellion, Leino had informed someone in the military about it. He and the president had arranged the transfer of a store of arms from under the Cathedral to a safer place. This happened on an agreed night. Now the minister was able say that he and the president had quelled the rebellion without any bloodshed. Among the Finnish communists, there was talk of his inefficiency in achieving a revolution. Maybe he felt it was better to be a communist in a free country than in charge of a commune elsewhere."

At this time, I had not looked into the reasons for Leino's departure from the party and loss of his wife. I felt sympathy for him as he was always alone, as I had been. I had the courage to sit at his table. My reason was gratitude. As Minister at the Home Office he had presented my application for Finnish Nationality. This happened after we lost the war, and he could have sent me back. Many were returned.

---

1 *YYA is a Finno-Soviet treaty 1948 agreement of friendship cooperation and mutual assistance*

A politician can outgrow his position, but how to replace him, was a question that can raise its head. You are chosen, because you are the right person for the job, but things can change - what then. The title of the job was high, it needed to be. After the war many evacuees had left their home and land, the question was how and where to settle the 400,000. Not an easy task. I was able as a journalist to observe: how land was allocated; the evacuees housed; and other problems solved - to the amazement of the world. The party wanted to sideline him, maybe the great land-owners did not want to share their land. When a civil servant has not broken any rules, he cannot be sacked easily. A new department was created and another man was to take the position. The first civil servant remained with a lower salaried position, and did not lose his privileges, but he has guaranteed the higher salary. So every year in the budget an amount was voted and passed. He kept his salary, probably index-linked. He left the party, started another one, dissolved the party or the party dissolved itself. He keeps going, where I am not aware.

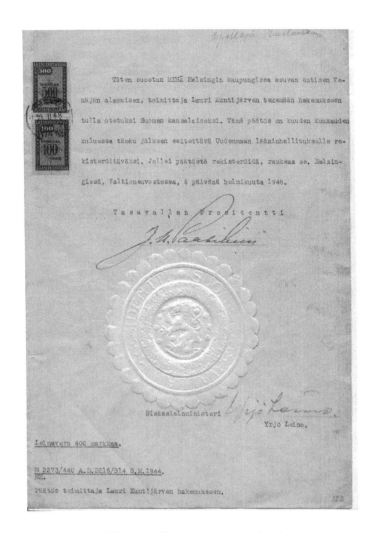

His Nationality acceptance paper, signed by President Paasikivi

Lähinnä edellisellä arkinsivulla oleva kansalaistamis-
päätös, joka koskee toimittaja Lauri Kuntijärveä, on tänään
Uudenmaan lääninhallituksessa rekisteröity, mikä täten todis-
tetaan.

Helsingissä, lääninkansliassa, helmikuun 26 päivänä
1948.

Maaherra _Väinö Meltti._

Lääninneuvos Y.J. Eskeli.

N:o A.856.

Leima 120:-.

A NEW BEGINNINg in education

My greatest work was probably the twelve years when I tried to improve the educational standards of the refugees, before and during the war. My aim was to increase the number of students to all possible levels - university, or vocational education.

Now it was my turn to experience the education field. My daughter, Kaarina, was to sit her exams for grammar school place. This was the first year, when primary school teachers could influence the results. Her old teacher felt that she should have grade 9 in Finnish language, but gave only 8, so that she would keep on trying. Sadly the teacher did not understand to significance of the points this year.

Her written test was to take place in a school where her two brothers were already studying. We needed to get our last child in but it was very crowded with the large numbers after the war 1944. We saw that her name was not on the list, Anni, Kaarina and me were all a little sad, perhaps even tearful. To be told that many other schools would have accepted her with the lower points, did not help.

Other schools would have accepted her because results were higher than needed. But the school we wanted had the brothers.

We could apply to one of these schools. Schools would normally search for a place, but this part had not been completed by the schools. This job would be a do-it-yourself job.

We went to the cottage. I was sitting in the bus gazing outside. My thoughts were about schools. It seemed outrageous that I had spent so many years building a system for the refugees to achieve a schooling and now apparently cannot do anything for my beloved child. The bus moved passed traffic lights and inspiration hit me. Schools are started by people, and when there is a need, one must act. There is a need, because over 2000 pupils in Helsinki alone, were left outside the grammar school door.

The next day I placed an advertisement in the Helsingin Sanomat about starting a new school. I made a mistake in placing my own phone number as the contact.

The country was short of money, it was 10 years after the end of war. They were debating an increase of child benefits in the parliament, communists using various delaying tactics - the amount was perhaps 200 marks. Sitting in the cafe of the parliament, I was furious about it. "Why don't you start more schools first and then increase the child benefit". In this heated discussion I had thrown the idea that if you put 100,000 per person and collect 1000 people who are interested, you have a school.

The idea was greatly helped by a lady[1] whose husband would buy 10 shares, which would be a million in old money. As a couple

---

1 *This lady was the aunt of Molla, who was Kaarina's bridesmaid and god mother to our son, Jari*

OPPIKOULUUN PYRKIVIEN
LASTEN VANHEMMILLE

Noin 2.000 oppikouluun hyväkuytyä lasta joutuu ensi syksynä uudelleen kilpailemaan n. 270 pulpetista. Ongelmaa ei ratkaista välmennuskursseilla eikä sillä, että kiistellään antaako pisteet kansakoulunopettaja vai oppikoulunopettaja. Se ratkaistaan järjestämällä lisää koulutiloja. Uuden oppikoulun perustamisesta kiinnostuneita vanhempia pyydetään ottamaan yhteys allekirjoittaneeseen.

LAURI KUNTIJÄRVI, toimittaja, puh. 44 62 27.

ADVERT FOR SCHOOL in Helsingin Sanomat June
1955

Is your child looking for a place this year.

About 2000 children who were accepted in the spring, will have to fight for approx. 270 desks. The problem is not solved by taking extra courses in the summer and who is giving the vital points. Is it the junior or the senior school teacher? It is solved by creating more school places. If you as a parent are interested in founding a new school, please contact undersigned.

Lauri Kuntijärvi telephone me xxxxxxxx

they were aware of army families having to move and children changing schools frequently. This could cause problems, no boarding schools here.

The idea developed, the money came, and somehow the school was organised. My mistake with school board was not asking the lady, who had 10 shares, to be a member of the board. A director of a airline was asked to be the chairman, I was forced to accept the vice chair. I had only planned to be active with the school for a year, and then move to my own work, which was not completed. I was continuously preaching a motto, people whose life is 'ready' will take the lead, I must still continue with my unfinished life.

Things progressed, but we had problems too. The Minister of Education, whom I had known well during my parliament time, did not grant the concession to open the school. She had not granted this to country schools, so we could not be an exception. We were advised to start as a kind of home school. This was done, but still under the umbrella of the National Board of Education and were inspected by them. I believe we had some help with teachers' salaries also. I discovered that schools could start new classes without permit, but to start a new school seem to need one. No permit, no new school.

Where to start? A school in Töölö, had some spare class rooms, but the head of the school was somewhere in Italy, holiday time. Found him, but the answer was no, they were needed by the school. New search resulted in an unusual place for the starting school. The Olympic Stadium built 1938, had the olympics 1952, and the classes started there. The school was going to need a different and a permanent place, a piece of land. This was a problem, we all had different ideas about the suitability, but eventually after several fights a piece of land was secured. It was

The first graduation group

noticeable, that old friendships, however high, did not help our cause. An architect and 'sackful' of money attracts more money, so we were able to start the building project. We had many experts, but apparently the first building was not so good, - it was only the second school in Finland to have air conditioning, was it necessary, probably not.

The teachers did not cause a problem, only two classes to start with, but to find a headmaster was another matter. I found many candidates - however the majority of the board were not willing to see them. Our current person was only a temporary solution, and we must have a permanent person. His papers contained something that was not acceptable, and even the president could not agree to his application to modify them. I wanted a headmaster who had a good reputation. A complaint procedure was the only way to allow a new candidate to come forward. The temporary head finally stepped aside, and we appointed a current member of the staff. I know this possibly damaged our reputation, but a good headmaster is vital for the students. My work at this time was really difficult, I did not want to alienate all the hard working people because of the quarrel about the headmaster, but to get a good result eventually was good.

My one year stretched to three years and having gallstones did not help. I was hanging on, had I left early, no one would have voted against it. Now it was suggested I could propose a vice chairman, and therefore leave. I don't think anyone was unhappy about it, for me it was also good. During this time six gallstones had made my world blacker than black and time for them to go too.

It was inevitable that newspapers would have a field day about the school. The evening tabloid was referring in an article about 'money buys everything', including a desk at the school. It was not mandatory to buy a share to get your child a desk, but maybe in practice a parent bought one to secure a place now or for the future. After the war and the increase in birthrates, places were scarce in schools. As the school was black marked in this way at the beginning, I had to make every effort to help its reputation, hence the dispute about the headmaster. Maybe the school had a mixture of pupils at the beginning, where standards varied greatly. Well in eight years time the results can be seen, the baccalaureate will show parents, critics and the country, if money bought the 'cap'.

I was interested in mixing the academic studies which lead to university and vocational studies together. I had seen this during my war years, that it could work, studying and working. A student would alternate these, perhaps even take time off from school, work and return to studies. I was aware that families were willing to pay a great deal of money for children's education and not complain. So all was well for grammar, co-educational schools, but vocational schools did not have enough pupils. Both parties could benefit, also vocational group would be ready to enter the work place but academics needed the university to obtain masters or doctorate enter the workplace and good earnings. Loans need to be paid back also, so student life is hard.

For this experimental plan, I had other ideas. It could be three terms. I was a friend of nature and children, so in the summer term the school could be outside, learning about nature, but also a language. We could bring children from other countries and a spoken language could happen naturally in this summer school. I even had a place for the summer school, a good place, which fell by the wayside as we had a more important question - the choice of the headmaster was gathering clouds over the horizon. Somethings are more important and timely, don't dream of next year when today's problems are in front of you.

We all could rejoice eight years later when our pupils passed the exams. Yes, number was not the same, but those who took it, passed well. My daughter was one them.

It took twenty years before I visited the school again. . . this was the final stages of the school about giving it up to the county. We, the original shareholders, were not informed correctly about the plans. Messy and undesirable result. I had share No.1 as a starter of the school, but new share issues had happened, and now somebody was voting with proxy, after collecting the shares from people. This can happen, but for a school it was the end.

A NEW PATH

Nurmijärvi, the home of Aleksis Kivi, who wrote the first important book[1] in the Finnish language, did not have a newspaper. Here was an opportunity. I thought that this town needed it's own newspaper. Life was changing: in the parliament both for the parties as well as the owners of papers. Some papers were leaning to the left which made me aware that a new path was in front of me. I was having dinner with a managing director, whose newspaper took my articles. During our conversation I happened to ask, "What do you need for printing a newspaper". He replied, "Printing press, typesetting machine and some large letters for headers". As they were buying a new one the old was available, so I purchased a printing press during our dinner. It was not expensive, and the rest I purchased later. My intention was to have the press at Nurmijärvi, but it seemed sensible to have it in Helsinki and deliver the paper to them.

---

1 *Next to Kalevala, Seven Brothers is the best known work of Finnish literature, even though Swedish was still the official language.*

I wanted to have people from the town involved in the enterprise. The headmaster was my first contact, a school with Christian principles, former tribal friend as well. He chose the rest of the "team", the bank manager, and a teacher who was to follow him as a headmaster in later years. I mentioned a dean, I had known and respected greatly, this he said will happen. We walked together like old friends to the first meeting, to arrange the legal and shareholding issues. I mentioned that fifty or even a quarter would be suitable for me. My friend said -"We are gentlemen so you can trust us".

I trusted. Shares were divided and each had a quarter. The newspaper would be printed in my printing works and a price was agreed. All this was agreed on a paper. Our operation started, it was shared, everybody would contribute in their best way. I wrote the first main column, but there is always a 'but'. The money from sales went to Nurmijärvi and I in Helsinki seemed to get all the invoices. Editions were produced until number 8 was printed - yet I had received no money. So it was time to demand payment.

Three men who had the shares with me, came to my office in Helsinki. Our meeting was painful, perhaps for all of us. They had found a place nearer to them and a cheaper price, I was not consulted. Outside the 'christian' said "we did a dirty trick on you", I replied "it does not matter". What else could I say. We drove to the printing works, where they took all the prepared material for issue number 10, and left. Later they paid. However, the final blow came when I was informed that my shares had 'disappeared' - there were now only three share holders. Where did my shares go? Later they found another person who made up the four.

ESPOON SANOMAT

Ilmestyy kaksi kertaa viikossa, tiistaisin ja perjantaisin.

Päätoimittaja
Lauri Kuntijärvi

Toimitus ja konttori:
Helsinki 10
Runeberginkatu 37 A 31

Puhelimet: 44 42 37, 49 52 21
Postisiirtotili: N:o 1218 25-7
Pankit: KOP Keski-Töölö
PYP Keski-Töölö

Ilmoitushinnat: Etusivu —:70
mm. tekstisivulla ja takasi-
vulla —:60 mm.

Kihlaus-, vihkimä- ja synty-
mäilmoitukset (20 mm) 5:—
Kuolinilmoitukset —:25 mm.

Tilaushinnat: 1/1 vsk. 12:—,
1/2 vsk. 7,20, 1/4 vsk. 4,20.

Kirjapaino: Tapiola ,
Ahertajantie 6, puh. 46 40 28

Tapio-Paino, Espoo 1971

I consulted my lawyer about taking the person to court - what could we accuse him of - that he had not done the paperwork after the first meeting?, and not filed the legal papers? or something else?.

My decision was that although he had swindled me I would not to take him to court. I could take the headmaster of a Christian school to court for breaking an agreement we made while standing by the church, exposing him as a swindler. However although this might have caused his reputation to suffer. It might also have impacted the school's reputation. In the end I decided to leave it to the afterlife and his day of judgement.

ESPOON SANOMAT

A printing shop needs work. It was situated in Espoo, so founding a newspaper for Espoo seemed a good idea. This time my partner was my wife Anni. We owned it for 15 years, it was published twice a week by us, and by the new owners only three times.

Here are my principles and basis of our work. When starting a new business at our age, the plan was not to create an empire, long lasting for our children, but one which would give us a secure retirement. This kind of entrepreneur will not look to borrowed capital, he will play it safely. We did not increase the circulation at any cost, but our plan was to get the necessary things slowly and surely. Machinery, and property were bought and the idea was to conquer the field, to increase the subscription base next. Our aim was not to borrow from the bank but to use our own capital. A proper business man plans differently, our age was the barrier for this action. So our plan worked well, unfortunately my partner did not have time to enjoy the proceeds, she passed away too early at sixty four.

Sometimes it is better not to say too much about your circulation and the field in which you have worked for 15 years, just remain silent. When a community starts and delivers a free paper, journalism is at its lowest and maybe also the society. Times change and I gave my paper and the printing press to my son, as I realised that I have plenty of Mammon and it ties you down. I will now have the peace and quiet to remember the past, and only include memorable stories which would not hurt anyone.

THE RESTAURANT CAR

When my wife bought the land at Rekola, it was classified for commercial use. I was still working as a journalist in the Diet (Parliament) and the owner of the news bureau where my main work was as a political journalist amongst other things. I noticed an advertisement in the paper about railway carriages, restaurant cars, which were made in Paris and brought to Finland at the turn of the century, six, were for sale. The price was not bad 1,200 marks (at that time) and it would seat forty two persons. I have a place for it, where the chickens lived all those years ago, could now become a restaurant. A summer place before could now become a money earner in our retirement.

As soon as I arrived at the parliament, I made a phone call to my wife. They are enchanting, wonderful work by Parisian and western European craftsmen. They were used here in Finland for half a century and fed the travellers in a grand way. Inside was untouched by time, so I asked Anni "Shall I buy?" "Why not, you sound really excited about it".

And my troubles really started, which are not over yet, but the worst is over. My strength and courage have diminished, and there are still problems to solve. My initial restaurant plan I did not and will not get. Maybe a train for a hermit, if it will ever be finished. First problem was how to transport this monster. We needed a heavy goods transporter to bring it from the railway depot to its final destination. The best route was a country road which included a low bridge, and a short sharp s-bend around an ancient barn. It had to be lifted over the bridge. It weighed 30,000 kg, and a crane which could lift a 50,000 kg weight was needed. A special permit was necessary from the authorities for the transportation. The thirty mile journey took a day and a night and cost more than the original purchase.

We forgot the problems, and the train stood on the plot, mine, to the horror of the local residents. Something must be done, the architect did a plan, and it was submitted to the first level of planning administration, next level and the next - and finally to the Home Office. My stumbling block was the County Architect, who had sent a letter to county departments forbidding any part of the train being used. Later I met him, we spoke about this train and now he was enthusiastic, and said they must be saved. However he was not helpful in the matter, despite his enthusiasm. This was the first time I was powerless in front of civil servants.

Maybe it was my own project that stopped me talking persuasively. It is easy to speak well about other people's cases, but not your own. I tried to use my connections, by talking to the Home Secretary. I simply said, my case will be next in highest law office in the land and then in the Home Office, maybe it could be dealt favourably. The minister, whom I knew well, nodded and was sure there would be a good result.

One week I noticed that the minister didn't stop for our usual chat and was hiding behind the pillars in the coffee place, before disappearing into chamber, where journalist are not allowed.

The restaurant car which was made in Paris about 1900

A letter arrived, denial again, signed by the minister and somebody, perhaps a civil servant, who said to me, we decide and the minister signs what we have decided. The first application was for a restaurant. Then it was changed to a house with a courtyard - atrium - and travelled the same route up to the Home Office, the answer was 'No'. I am tired and fed up with the civil service, its different departments and government which is controlling and stopping individual efforts. No authority only civil servants.

I let it lie for ten years. It deteriorated and was raped. One winter night, someone broke in and stole the beautiful copper coat hangers. He had taken the lights and shades and placed them on top of a cupboard. I visited later and saw the lamps, and stole them back. A real thief is one who steals from the original thief. Later, they used a saw to cut the copper heating pipes and took them away. At that moment I felt that my soul had been cut and taken away in pieces. The police came, and suggested that I should put out traps. When I asked about this being legal, the younger one replied 'I don't care one way or another. To catch them I would use any sort of trap!' They saw a foot print in the copper dust from the cutting of the pipes. It was big - like Yetis'. Ten years have passed and they did not return - there was nothing left to take.

A miracle happened. The locals signed a petition that something must be done with the train. I replied that although I have made two attempts to get planning permission, I am prepared to try again. I submitted the same application again to the council - and I received permission. My son, Veikko who was a qualified civil engineer, took the task on. He drew the plans and supervised the building work. Finally when it was ready, it became a Post Office, the wish of the Minister. Better late than never.

Designed and completed by my son, Veikko.
Recycling from Restaurant Car to Post Office

NOW I LIVE ALONE

Our journeys continue, often quietly and at difficult times would we be silent. This is when you notice, sulking, or moping, will not get you anywhere. So work continues. I notice that we, people, gather many things, unnecessary items, perhaps for prestige or other reasons. So we fill our lives with junk and stuff and often have no space to keep them. Our wishes were filled, but one more push, which was too much. The doctor said to come, a few weeks in hospital care, and she improved and believed a better time was coming. What is better place, nobody knows, but I believe she is there.

I am alone, and as I look at the old handbag, I could see the small amount of money, which she could produce in a crisis moment. Also the pound notes left from our trip to our daughter's wedding in England were still there. Memories, she died at midsummer 1974. I was going to buy her a new fur coat - we had not had a trip in the new boat, I know for her this is not a regret, she was not a boat person.

Anni was born in Finland, but her family originally came from Uhtua, which is in Karelia. Many people changed their name and religion when they escaped to Finland. Her surname was Sergejeff and religion Russian Orthodox, like mine was Kundozeroff, but I never changed to Lutheran religion, which caused some problems later. Our children were not named in the orthodox church register.

The Karelian club was a meeting place, where singing and dancing and of course my speeches were the norm. So we met, I was also keen on the theatre, which was next to my school. The price was right if you were prepared to sit in the gods, we met there as well. My whole life seemed to be full of ideology for Karelia and how to improve their life in this country. There was no time for anything else, not even love. However over many weeks, Anni was helping in the office, she was shy but her work was excellent, and we worked together very well. Our life later on was also like a working partnership.

After all this work and late nights, I decided to take Anni to theatre, but this time we had seats to match the occasion, the play was perhaps irrelevant, and during the break we even ventured to the foyer to have a coffee. I noticed how pretty she was, and the play finished, but we continued our meetings, working and social events. The summer festivals and so one day we walked to Sundqist's jeweller and bought the rings.

I lived another 14 years, in the same place in Töölö where I had lived most of my life in Helsinki. The boat harbour was a walking distance, the swimming club was further, but I persevered at least twice a week, even in the coldest of weathers. Sauna afterwards and a cup of coffee with a bun was the norm, and then walk back home - about a mile away. My boat was important, like my child-

*A big smile for all to see. On a boat, fishing, and enjoying one of his grand children.
A wonderful day in his retirement.*

hood times, now with a motor, so I could go far. And buy some fish, if I did not catch any. I remember Anni saying a few times, when the fish was bought from a shop, "the fish was a little old". How did she know? The fishmonger had asked about the fish - "Was it good, your husband and a friend bought one yesterday". I was caught.

Later Anni's family asked us, the children, to stop the boat trips. He was using a walking stick and somehow getting into the boat that would swing dangerously. Our reply was simple "Have you ever tried to ask him not to do something?". We did not, and so he happily continued his boat trips.

This is the end of his biographical text. Time to examine the contents of the box.

It gave us the text of his biography, We published it together with as much documentation that we could find in 2018.

"Tuhat Rautaa Tulessa" is availabe from the SKS website.

Kaarina spent the whole of lockdown translating his text, and together we have made this book for Jari, family and friends.

The box also had the names and addresses of relatives living in Karelia. We tried to follow up on them, went to the Military Archives and libraries in Helsinki. And we visited his relatives.

But the box also contained a few letters that reveal his inner self, and why - despite having respect and friendship from people, former pupils and his wife's relatives - he labelled his last chapter "I live alone".

K & D

WE START OUR RESEARCH

In addition to his family, the box has dozens of letters and documents - and a typewritten manuscript of his biography. It is from these sources that we learn just what an incredible life he lead. But the translation has been difficult. We wish to make his life understandable to the readers. But it is made harder because of the time lapse between the years, and the geographical differences between our lives here in Britain in the 2020's and the lives in a tiny village on the outskirts of the Arctic Circle at a period when the communist USSR was being developed, and the world under the threat of nuclear war. How can we help todays young to understand how difficult it was to succeed in those times.

These were times that we lived through here in the UK. Yet, Lauri lived in the same era in Finland. His birth family in Karelia, though living through the same years, were living in a country going through the bolshevic and communist turmoil. Cut off from the world - alone making his way in a democracy with quite different ways, laws, etc.

Despite which, he succeeded in a number of projects that made him known in many parts of Finland. Just the day after his death was

140

announced, a dear friend said "They'll know it right across the country". His children were incredulous. "Why? He is just our dad".

Lazarus Kundozeroff was never 'just' anything.

Our journey to his family and Soukelo

It is post glasnost when we return to the letters in the box that Kaarina found after Lauri's funeral in 1988. They are dated 1967 - while the iron curtain was impenetrable. Among them are the four letters from the family in Karelia, pinned together by Lauri, and shown in the following pages. Now that the iron curtain has been lifted we might be able to visit Karelia. Over a number of years, we had wondered if we should try to go? We had many questions, and finally decided to at least try.

A window of opportunity opened in the summer of 2000. David was due to retire, and the KSS was organising a language course for Finns and Karelians to be held in a school in Kiestinki. Not a place associated with any of the family, but if we registered ouselves on the course we would be part of an 'official' group travelling in Russia with the protection this offerred. No, we might not meet the family, but perhaps one of them could travel to the course? And at the least we will have seen the countryside and get an idea of what his life may have been.

We decided to try, and wrote to every address we could glean from the 1967 family letters. Perhaps we might get a reply?

We got an avalanche of letters from different parts of Karelia eager to regain contact. (Well about 7, but it seemed like an avalanche.)

One was from a relative who is an interpreter living in Murmansk. She had tried to find information about Lauri on her visits across the border in Finland, but had only got the news that he was married and had three children - nothing else. All of this was unknown to us until the funeral in 1988. Okay, let's do it!

We went through all the hoops - a story in itself - and ended up at the border, very excited, full of visas, vaccines, special insurances, euros and roubles.

Kaarina relates the story

I am Kaarina, Lauri's daughter and this is what I remember of the visit to his family and village.

"It is mid-summer in the year 2000 and we are standing at a border[1] between Finland and Russia. It is our gap year and we are 55 and 60 years old. It is a momentous time. Four letters stapled together from January 1967 have brought us here. A letter, not a modern computer message like a Whats App, but an old fashioned letter between two people and two countries.

We meet a relative (Svetlana) and her husband (Leo) at the Finnish side of the border. (We had to use the international border crossing at Vartius) We had never met before and will have language difficulties but a connection is made. They will help us, but there is a problem. When applying for the visa in Helsinki, we were asked to check that information was correct. It was, but the pronunciation caused a misunderstanding. To resolve the issue a higher ranking border official was called. He put his hand forward and in my ignorance I shook it. There was a silence. You could hear a pin drop. We were asked into a separate room. This is it, what will happen next, and were will it lead? He had only wanted our passports to look at. My cousin Svetlana and husband Leo spoke to him at length in Russian and the situation was cleared.

We proceed into their car, our car remains at the Finnish border, and drive 10 meters to Russian customs. We have ready our passports and a completed form which we were told is necessary for passing into Russia, and later for leaving. "Very important" we had been told. It listed everything, money camera etc. Trying to pass it to the cus-

---

1 Vartius is an international crossing

toms officer, Svetlana indicated not necessary, put it away. The officer took one look at Leo and settled down to continue reading his newspaper. We believed her. Once on the other side we are led into the building and upstairs into the office of the senior Customs Officer on duty. What now?

"Take a photo", Svetlana suggested. A pregnant silence. David knew about ´customs´ and he simply opened the camera and showed it had no film. Smiles all round and we were taken to view the direct link between here and Moscow, returned to the office for coffee, given gifts, and we drove away from the border in Leo's car. Phew! After driving about two or three kilometers we came up to a barrier across the road. A soldier came to us and Leo opened his window. He handed out four paper tokens and answered a few questions - deferentially. The soldier grudgingly opened the barrier and we proceeded. Quite a different atmosphere from the Customs Office. Strange?

As we drove along the deserted road away from the border, we noticed that there were tall watch towers, and one had someone in it with a pair of binoculars trained on our car. What are they watching? We later discover that Leo is a very high ranking customs officer at the border. Maybe we were given a red carpet treatment because of him. But elsewhere, he has no sway. So all is well after initial difficulties - provided we take no liberties!

At Svetlana and Leo's flat, we tell that we are to be collected tomorrow and will drive north to Kiestinki, the town where the course will be held. Our first day is good and next day, we will leave them to go to the language course.

We are picked up by Sakari. He is a seasoned traveller who crosses the border a couple of times a month and knows what is needed. Driving on the various roads was an experience. Who would believe that we helped with road works in Karelia? Our car was a powerful four wheel drive which helped to spread the sand delivered to the *middle of the road for repair work. It was the custom. The sand was left for traffic to do the actual work.*

Stopped for lunch in Uhtua at a relative's house, except it seems strange that all of us are related somehow. Uhtua was a larger place, and was where my Mother's family came from. Lunch and driving continued to our destination.

We arrive at another barrier inside Karelia, a barrier stopping internal traffic in both directions. Stop the car, "Stay in", is the request from Sakari and we hand out our passports. A young guard looks at one, the next and a third, and takes all five quickly into the building. We wind the windows up because of mosquitoes. It is hot and we wait, maybe ten minutes. He comes back smiling and the barrier is lifted for us now. The traffic had moved well all the time we were waiting for approval of our passports. Sakari now hands the young man a packet of cigarettes, not before because it could have looked like a bribe. Our journey was twelve hours and our bodies ached despite the excellent car. We had averaged 19-20km per hour!

We met the Karelian family where we were to stay for the six days of the course, and given the best room in the house - which did not have many rooms. Gave a present to our host. I had been told to bring suitable gifts to every house we might visit. How to do this was difficult. How many houses and we did not know any of them, and room in the luggage is limited. So I had a brilliant idea, Lauri would return to his home country in the form of the book which he wrote in Karelia during the Continuation War. I had to find more copies because I only had two and needed at least five. Sakari Vuoristo, the Editor-in-Chief of Karjalan Heimo, came to the rescue and so Lauri, my father, returned home in the form of the book which he wrote in 1943.

The course was interesting. Karelian language course for teachers, who wanted to teach it in Karelia at the schools. The teacher was Pekka Zaikow, whose grandmother was my grandmother's sister. At the moment I didn't even know my grandmother's name. Later when we meet my father's cousin who is about 90 years old, I am told her name. The old lady remembers Lauri and said he was a nice boy. Jevdokia was my Karelian grandmother.

The course was attended by a lady who wanted the book for her father. Fine. I gave her a copy. Little did I know that she was involved in the Ministry of Minority Languages and later requested permission to reprint the book in Karelian. Permission given and fortunately I found the paperwork at home for original contract, so I have not broken the law of contract. Book was printed and my son Jari helped me to transfer the money whilst we were sitting in St Thomas Hospital (2005) - David had just had the strokes and was unable do so. I am not the most computer literate and transferring money whilst worrying about my husband was beyond me.

I am rambling on a little but it is all part of the bigger picture. The course finished and we are given a certificate, probably for attendance. We were unlikely ever to teach the language. For David it was hard, it was in Karelian and Russian perhaps Finnish but no English unless I spoke to him.

This time my faux pas was with the headmaster at this school. We met him in the class room which was for English lessons. He must believe us to be very wealthy. Their photocopier had broken, and could we replace it with a new one. The amount was far too much to even consider it. The English teacher came in and I shook hands with her, but noticed she was totally ignored by the men in the room. Women obviously are invisible and I was one them, but I could be a soft touch and give money to the school. We mentioned English books, we would be very happy to send some, headmaster promptly said, "there is no need for that!".

Svetlana and Leo arrive to continue our journey north. More relatives and someone has travelled from Murmansk twelve hours to meet us. A place with a sauna and a greenhouse which must be 24 feet long and 6 feet wide. Produce is needed for the winter and shops of course are not next door. In the kitchen I notice a sackful of flour. Later we do some cooking together and because there is an accordion David wanted play. Everybody was very happy and I think vodka was flowing too.

A boat journey has been arranged to the place where father and family had lived. Some years ago the area was flooded, because hydro power was needed for the country. It was a long journey and only a small island is now visible. Moored and men fished, we made some fish soup and tried to eat. To eat wearing a mosquito hat over your head is a challenge. I took some water in a bottle and some sand, pulled out a small fir tree to take back to Finland. My motive was to bring some of his country back to his grave. Water and sand succeeded, but I think the fir trees died.

Now only a few days left and we return to Svetlana's flat, but they wanted to show us the typical dacha (summer house, that many families have) and visit was arranged. By now David was more than ready to leave, I am in the middle of it all, language again. We drive there and it is charming, had a sauna stayed the night and then back to flat. Leaving next day, but must go through the same border crossing we used earlier. Now we are all nervous, that piece of paper Svetlana said was not necessary, suddenly is important to Leo. There had been a problem because a member of the Finnish government was not allowed to use a different crossing earlier in the week. Fortunately we get through and find our car still at the Finnish side. My family in Finland was nervous, we were late returning and there had been an incident between the two countries. A Diplomatic Note was exchanged between the countries and everybody's imagination can play havoc and we were late. All is well that ends well."

A valuable trip to the Archives

He was born in Soukelo, but exactly when, he was unsure. The Russian Orthodox church was responsible for registering all the dates of births, deaths and marriages. These significant dates were remembered by the villagers until the Orthodox priest made a visit and recorded them.

We were able to arrange a visit to the archives in Petroskoi where the church registers were kept. Kaarina´s 2nd cousin, Svetlana, was allowed go in. She found his entry and also found his parents´ marriage record. We asked for copies and had a heated discussion about the cost amounting to about two weeks wages. Very expensive for them. We explained that the cost will be shared by our family in Helsinki. Finally it was agreed and we returned the next day to collect them.

The date, however, was different to all other dates recorded by various authorities in Finland:
when he arrived in Kuusamo, he declared an older age so that he would not be returned - we don't have the details;
the army record shows 20/4/1906;
the Governor´s permit at Kemi shows 20/4/1909;
Petroskoi archives show birth 14/4/1907, baptism 20/6/1907

This is not the end of the problem. The earliest Christian calendar was Julian, but a revised calendar, Gregorian, varied from the older by thirteen days. It was introduced and adopted by the catholic countries. England adopted it in 1752 and Sweden in 1753. (Finland was under Sweden then). Russia did not adopt the new calendar until 1918. At the time Russia "lost" 13 days. Two weeks were just written off. Do not exist in history. This was simply done overnight.

Because Lauri´s record was entered in 1907, this date was from the Julian calendar, which he used when responding to the Finnish. We have changed his record by adding 13 days to Julian to become Gregorian in the family tree, but his tombstone still has the old

147

SOME OF THE Correspondence

Dear brother Miihkali[1] (An extract of Lauri's letter)

1950-51?

So good to hear from you, a genuine letter is as welcome as the person who wrote it. It would be so great to share our old times and the stories relating to those times. You wanted know about my current job. Outi's[2] description about my work was correct. I write a lot, I go to the parliament, I blame and thank our statesmem and there are mountains of newspapers in my room. I am also able to share, if there is no conflict, my stories with magazines as well as various other newspapers, not just ones I have a contract with.

It is my job to follow the hustle and bustle of Parliament, and because of this I have a chair reserved in the Press gallery. I know about 10 out of 15 ministers so well in the current governement, that I can use the informal you (which is in Finnish 'sinä' not 'te' in French 'tu' not 'vous').

I am known in these circles as a man of progress but always impartial. I have proved a handy expert in political intrigue. Interviewing some people is hard in any language, so have started also to learn Swedish and English again. However to reach a competent level is beyond to reach a level which would be of practical use.

---

1 Mikko Karvonen

2 Mikko's wife

My final revelation is, that I seem to have some kind of position among the Helsinki journalists and statesmen. I like my job. It is the best I have ever had and my earnings have improved a bit, but still I am and will always be poor, really poor.

The fact that Väinölä was taken from the war orphans by devious means hurts, I am one myself. This is a course worth fighting again, but perhaps not.

I am alone spiritually, not interested in anyone. For sake of my office I go to all the necessary events, the opening and closing of the Parliament etc, but there are no old friends, who share the spirit. You are there and Aksola[1]. I meet him sometimes and we have fun. The only place I live a full life is at my plot in Rekola, where I am building a cottage. The basement will be ready before Korean War expands and soon cellar also. I was coming to see you but money and time has gone to building work. The basement is the best place during wars, I will stay there if necessary. That is my lesson.

Well put pen to paper when you get the letter....Lasse

Dear brother Miihkali   (An extract of Lauri's letter) 4/3/1977

---

1 at Loppi not far from Helsinki and a headmaster of a school

I have something interesting to tell you. Last week a student, researcher, telephoned and asked if he could interview me about East Karelian Military Administration. He mentioned that a collection of papers did not contain anything about Advisory Board. I laughed and said "Not surprised, the papers are in Sweden".

This was enough for him now, but I promised to be in touch with the keeper of the papers. It will be possible when archives are freely available for researchers. I believe that Advisory Board's work should also become known. He had better lists of names of members, which I did not know (although I was there). He knew about Nordström who had monopoly when there was a choice of military personnel (AKS came first). He had read the minutes of a meeting requested by Military Administration at Enso-Gutzeit offices. Kotilainen, our first commendant was there (take nitro for heart). Maybe you remember him. If there was need to talk, this was done over a dinner, but nothing was written down! This was at his request or command. The minutes had a very strong words about Advisory Board's work.

Reporting many things amongst them was we only criticise, use old information and so on. He had read a great deal about all of it. I said that they (military) did good things with the education, but there were many things we could not agree. This includes religion, giving Vako monopoly over retail, wage policy and helping locals with cultural work. His papers had many questions about Vuokkiniemi meeting. I personally feel that on this occasion we could correct the wrong information about us (AdvisoryBoard, not you and me). The military can conceal if nothing is written about meetings. I always felt this was wrong.

Life is busy. Went to the Finnish Cultural Association annual event. Even had a companion. The event had a dress code, tails mandatory. I count how many of my age group attend, and numbers are getting lower.

I attended the 'last moments' of the school I founded. I was to vote with my share and other people's shares by proxy. It was private school, but no more.

I feel fairly well, swim twice a week, walk and company is invigorating. I am going to England to see Kaarina, but here, I also need to keep an eye on the boys. Veikko and others are now running the business. Many problems there, some people are not business men, Antero is good with practical side but not for leading the company. I have stepped aside, but!!!

My best regards to Outi and family. Hope your hospital visit goes well.

Lasse

The correspondence between Lauri and Jouki

Extract of Jouki's letter   12/1/67

I don't know you but was able to read your letter. I am Jouki.
Daughter of your sister Stepania. I want tell about us and
find out about your family. Hope you can understand my
letter, it is very difficult for me write in Finnish. Your sister
Uljana has died, also your brother Leontei 1936. Vaseli was
killed in the war. My mother died 1949, only your youngest
sister Hekla is alive. Stepania had 5 children and we are all
married, Three girls and two boys.

I am the only one in Kiestinki. I have a husband and two
children, both still at school. We work. I will only write little,
and if I have a reply will write more. Photograph of your
family would be nice, I would like to look at you. My family
sends thousand greetings. I would be happy to get a reply.
My address is: Kostamus.

Lauri's reply   24/1/67

Dear relatives Jouki and family. I received your friendly
letter and I thank you. Also thank your country's post office
for delivering the letter I sent to my sister Uljana to your
address. I was given her address from Karelian connection.
They had a letter with her address, so the contact.

Your letter told me that in 44 years' separation many things have happened. We were seven children, but five have died and only two are alive, Hekla there and me here. I lit five candles for their memory that night.

I would be happy, if I could have Hekla's address so that I can write to her. Also when did Uljana die and do you know anything about Okahvie.

We are five, me, Anni my wife, daughter Kaarina eldest son Antero and next in line is Veikko. They are not married yet, but Kaarina is getting married to an Englishman. She is now in England preparing for the wedding this summer. Veikko studied at university and is a civil engineer, Antero looks after our printing works. I founded a newspaper and printing works.

You wanted a family photograph. Many photos, but not a family one. Finally found one at our summer house which I enclose with the letter, also a picture of the summer house. We live in Helsinki during the winter months. Hope to send a better family picture when Kaarina returns from England. We would also like to have pictures of you and family. Best regards to you Jouki, family and all the relatives who are there.

Your uncle Lauri

Address: Kuntijärvi Lauri, Väinämöisenkatu 15 A 26, Helsinki 10

Kiestinki 7/2/67

Hello uncle Lauri and all the family. I was very happy to receive your letter. I can now tell you more about your family here. You are our only uncle, but here you have many relatives. One brother lives in Leningrad but no family, eldest sister has seven children and my brother also, seven. They live at village of Niska. Last war made him totally blind. We suffered a lot during this war. Levontei, you brother has three daughters, who are married with children. One of his sons was killed in the war and one drowned. Vaseli married and has two daughters and a boy. All are married and live not far from me. I visited Hekla last year. After reading your letter I forwarded it to her and said we are corresponding. She has not replied, perhaps visiting her sons, who live elsewhere. Hekla's husband died two years ago. They had five children who are all grown up. Okahvie your sister is alive but not her husband. Five children also. I do not have her address. I have never seen her.

Thank you very much for your photograph. I have none now, because I have given all away to family and friends. One picture only of me and my husband. I also wanted to know, if you feel sorry for Kaarina who will live so far away?

The picture had a car outside your summer cottage. Is it your own car? This summer we want build a bigger house, but much money is needed, so maybe it is not possible.

My husband wanted to know, if you fish during the summer and is there a lake? We use fishing lines only because fishing nets us younger generation do not have the skills anymore. My mother was very good at it. Dear uncle could you get some Finnish carding needles, I keep sheep. We knit woollies, and also make cloth for men's trousers. I do not have good carding needles.

I want to send my best greetings to your family from us. Also Arhippa Lukeria from Soukelo if you still remember her. She came to see your picture. Now just goodbye and I will hope for a reply.

Jouki from your large Karelian family

Helsinki 8/6/1967

Dear Jouki

Thank you for your letter. It was a very good letter telling about many of my relatives. There are so many of you. So many young ones, we have only three children and us oldies, no grandchildren yet.

Kaarina is the first to get married. The wedding will take place in England 29 July this year. We will travel 15 of July and return in August. Of course we will miss her, but you can fly there in 3 hours. Flying is cheaper and quicker than by sea. We three fly together and I will come back with Anni.

You asked about the car, is it our own. Yes, and our son, who is an studying engineering at university, has his own car. Two cars, not an affluent or wealthy family, only a small entrepreneur. I have a motor boat, which will take me to the open sea. Tell your husband my warmest greetings and say that I have many tools and ways of fishing but do not fish much yet. Maybe later when I retire and have time.

I have managed to get carding needles for you[1]. Perhaps not the best but I will send what I was able to get. Also a fishing net. He needs put weights at the bottom the and top will need a float (to keep the net on the surface of water). I am sure Lukeria will still remember how to place the items on the top and bottom of the net for floating. My regards to Lukeria, I remember her very well. Many people from Soukelo are here but getting old.

Many have died. Of Harriman family, Risto has died, Seredin family all men have also died. Ontto, Jussi and Sakari. Family Tiittala - Iivo and Jaakko - are married and have a family.

You wrote about building. Has the work began? I should start, but feel old and don't really want do any more. I always admire people who build.

---

1 *The carding needles were not in use, but still held by the family. However the net was confiscated by the authorities of the commune.*

You mentioned about sheep. We had some chickens here at the cottage, but not now.

I will send the fishing net and carding needles in two parcels. The salesman said that the net was a very good one, so we must believe him

My best greetings to your family, all the relatives and Lukeria from my family here.

Lauri Kuntijärvi (he amended this to be "your uncle Lauri", to make it less formal).

*Above is the Orthdox Register. Lauri is the third entry.
The Finnish translation gives dates of birth April 14th,
baptism June 20th which is also the date registered.*

KIRKONKIRJA, VUOSI 1907,

Syntyneiden lasku		Kuukausi ja päivä		Syntyneiden nimet	Vanhempien sääty, etu-, isännimi, sukunimi ja uskonto
Miespuoliset	Naispuoliset	Syntymä	Kaste		
		Kesäkuu			
16	..	Huhtikuu 14.	20.	Lasar	Kemin kihlakunnan, Olangan kunnan, Sokolozeron yhteisön, Sokolozeron kylän talonpoika Mefodij Jevsejev Kundozerov ja hänen laillinen puolisonsa Jevdokija Rodionova, kumpikin ortodokseja. Pappi Leonid Vladimirov Shilov.

*Copy authorised by (on reverse)
National Archives in Petroskoi, Karelia
Originals in Old Church Russian*

Sisu is a unique Finnish concept. It is a Finnish term that can be roughly translated into English as strength of will, determination, perseverance, and acting rationally in the face of adversity.

Sisu is not momentary courage, but the ability to sustain that courage. It is a word that cannot be fully translated.

He was an extraordinary man, deserving the description "Sisu"